AFRICA

BY
HEIDI M.C. DIERCKX, Ph.D.

Copyright © 1998 Mark Twain Media, Inc.

ISBN 1–58037–089–6

Printing No. CD–1316

Mark Twain Media, Inc., Publishers
Distributed by Carson-Dellosa Publishing Company, Inc.

Table of Contents

Introduction

The nineteenth-century European belief that all in Africa was savage, barbaric, uncivilized, and chaotic before the Europeans explored and conquered the continent is considered a big misconception among African historians today.

"Far from being a kind of Museum of Barbarism whose populations had stayed outside the laws of human growth and change through some natural failing of inferiority, Africa is now seen to possess a history which demands as serious an approach as that of any other continent."

—Basil Davidson, *Africa in History*, p. 3

In fact, unlike some continents, most notably the Americas and Australia, Africa north of the Sahara belonged to the urban civilization of Islam. In Africa, south of the Sahara Desert (known as sub-Saharan Africa), evidence indicates the existence of a number of political entities, advanced in their administration and social structure, exploiting their own natural resources and trading with other Africans.

Africa was not as backwards as the Europeans claimed. Africa had different cultural values and was simply not as technologically advanced as Europe and Asia.

This book includes a variety of activities that will lead students to a better understanding of the rich cultural heritage of Africa and the fascinating history of the many African civilizations. Included are **Challenge** questions, which can serve as a review of the information presented in each narrative section. **Points to Ponder** are more in-depth questions that can serve as discussion or essay topics. **Map Activities** encourage students to locate the political entities and physical features presented to them in the narratives, thus allowing them to visualize the scope of those entities and the interactions between ethnic and national groups.

Time Line of African History

South Africa

1492	Portuguese round Cape of Good Hope
last half of 17th C.–19th C.	Dutch settle and expand
1652	Dutch East India Company settles at Cape of Good Hope; first Cape Colony
1746	Afrikaner Republic of Swellendam founded
1786	Afrikaner Republic of Graaf Reinet founded
1779	Beginning of expansion wars against Africans, "Kaffir Wars"; last about 100 years
1806	British seize Cape Colony from the Dutch
1800–1808	Military state of the Nguni Zulu formed
1818–1828	Reign of Shaka Zulu
1834	British abolish slavery in Cape Colony
1836–1854	"Great Trek" of Boers; expansion northwards
1838	Foundation of Republic of Natal
1843	British annex Natal province
1852	Afrikaner Republic of Transvaal founded
1854	Afrikaner Republic of Orange Free State founded
1867	Discovery of diamonds
1878	British are defeated by the Zulu at Isandhlwana
1890–1896	Cecil Rhodes is prime minister of Cape Colony; establishment of the British South Africa Company (BSA); BSA penetrates into the lands north of the Limpopo and Zambezi Rivers (Southern Rhodesia and Zambia)
1899–1902	Anglo-Boer War; Peace of Vereeniging
1910	Union of South Africa
1912	African National Congress founded (ANC)
1913	Natives Land Act
1919	Union of South Africa receives "mandate" authority for South West Africa (Namibia)
1923	Southern Rhodesia white settlers achieve self-rule as nominal Crown Colony of United Kingdom
1948	National Party wins elections; Apartheid system legalized
1951	South African "homelands" established
1960	Independence of Madagascar
1964	Nelson Mandela tried and jailed
1966	Independence of Lesotho and Botswana
1968	Independence of Swaziland
1977	Steve Biko assassinated

1980	Independence of Southern Rhodesia; received new name of Zimbabwe
1986	State of emergency declared in South Africa
1989	F.W. de Klerk becomes prime minister
1990	Nelson Mandela is released and takes control of the ANC; Independence of Namibia from South Africa
1994	End of Apartheid; Nelson Mandela elected president of South Africa
1997	National Party dissolves in South Africa

Central and East Africa

c. 400 B.C.–A.D.900	Bantu migrations
c. A.D.1000–1500	"Great" Zimbabwe Civilization
c. 1300	Foundation of Kingdom of Kongo
c. 1300–1600	Height of Swahili Culture
1483	Portuguese land on central African coast
16th and 17th C.	Portuguese raid and invade east and west central African coasts; Swahili city-states decline
1505	Portuguese seize Swahili cities
1506	Mani Kongo (Alfonso I) of Kongo converts to Christianity
1520s	Alfonso I of Kongo complains against slave traders
1607	Dutch East India Company seizes Portuguese Indian Ocean trade
1650s	Oman (Arabia) expels Portuguese and extends influence into Swahili cities
1698	Oman drives Portuguese out of Mombasa; east coast slavery prospers
1785	Oman takes control of Kilwa
1880–1914	Scramble for Africa
1884–1885	Berlin Conference
1908	Belgium assumes control of the Congo
1942–1945	World War II in Africa
1960	Independence of Chad, Congo, Gabon
1961	Independence of Rwanda and Tanganyika
1962	Independence of Uganda and Burundi
1963	Independence of Kenya
1964	Independence of Malawi; Tanganyika and Zanzibar become known as Tanzania
1965	Mobutu Sese Seke takes power in Congo
1966	Central African Republic declared
1971	Congo renamed Zaire
1975	Independence of Mozambique and Angola
1977	Independence of Djibouti
1993	Independence of Eritrea from Ethiopia

West Africa

c. 2500 B.C.	Desiccation of Saharan Region
c. A.D.1000/1100	Islam penetrates sub-Saharan Africa
c. 1100–1500	State of Benin
c. 400–1230	Rise of Ghana Kingdom
900-1180	Empire of Ghana
1180-1230	Decline of Ghana
1054	Almoravid Berbers take capital of Ghana
c. 1230–1450	Empire of Mali
c. 1230–1255	Reign of Sundiata
c. 1312–1337	Reign of Mansa Musa
c. 1375	Rise of Songhai power; raid of Niani
c. 1450–1600	Empire of Songhai at Gao
c. 1464–1492	Reign of Sonni Ali
1591	Moroccan invasion of Songhai
c. 1450-1870	Transatlantic slave trade
c. 1100-1846	Empire of Kanem-Bornu
1100-1575	Kanem Empire
1575-1846	Empire of Kanem-Bornu
c. 1100-1897	Benin State
1680-1800s	Ashante States
1804	Uthman dan Fodio proclaims Fulani jihad against the Hausa
1847	Republic of Liberia established
1880–1914	Scramble for Africa
1884–1885	Berlin Conference; partition of Africa
1942–1945	World War II in Africa
1957	Independence of Ghana
1958	Independence of Guinea
1960	Independence of Nigeria, Cameroon, Ivory Coast, Benin, Togo, Burkina Faso, Senegal, Niger, Mali, Mauritania
1961	Independence of Sierra Leone
1965	Independence of Gambia
1974	Independence of Guinea-Bissau
1975	Independence of Cape Verde
1967–1970	Nigerian civil war
1982–1989	Civil War in Chad

North Africa

3100–332 B.C.	Egyptian Civilization
c. 1000/900–600 B.C.	Kushite kingdom centered at Napata
751–663 B.C.	Kushite kings rule Egypt
332 B.C.	Conquest of Egypt by Alexander the Great
c. 300 B.C.	Ptolemaic Kingdom of Egypt
30 B.C.	Conquest of Egypt by the Romans
c. 600 B.C.–A.D. 330	Meroitic Kingdom of Kush
50 B.C.–A.D. 50	Height of Meroitic Kingdom
c. A.D. 100-900	State of Axum
A.D. 200-700	Height of Axum
A.D. 330	Axum conquest of Meroe
A.D. 622	Hijra of Islam; beginning of Islamic calendar
c. A.D. 570–632	Prophet Mohammed
A.D. 632-661	First phase of Islamic expansion
A.D. 661–750	Second phase of Islamic expansion; Ummayad Dynasty
A.D. 750–1258	Abbasid Dynasty
A.D. 969–1171	Fatimid Dynasty rules Egypt
1050s–1117	Berber Almoravids take Morocco
1140s–1250	Berber Almohads take the Maghreb region
13th and 14th C.	Portuguese begin voyages along northwest coast
1517	Ottoman Turks conquer Egypt
1830	Formal French rule proclaimed in Algeria
1859	Construction begins on Suez Canal
1869	Suez Canal opens
1881	France takes Tunisia
1882	British-French Protectorate in Egypt
1900	Italy takes control of Libya
1952	Gamal Abdul Nasser seizes power in Egypt; British withdraw
1954–1962	Civil War in Algeria
1956	Independence of Sudan, Morocco, Tunisia
1960	Independence of Somalia
1962	Independence of Algeria
1967	Israel invades Egypt in the "Six-Day War"
1969	General Qaddafi seizes power in Libya
1975	Western Sahara partitioned between Morocco and Mauritania
1976	Ethiopia-Somali War
1983	Sudan civil war begins
1990	Somalia civil war begins

List of African Countries, Capitals, and Dates of Independence

Country	Capital	Independence date (won from)
North Africa		
Algeria	Algiers	1962 (France)
Egypt	Cairo	1952 (Britain)
Libya	Tripoli	1951 (Italy)
Morocco	Rabat	1956 (France)
Tunisia	Tunis	1956 (France)
Western Sahara	El Aaiún	1976/1982 (Spain)
West Africa		
Benin	Porto-Novo	1960 (France)
Burkina Faso	Ouagadougou	1960 (France)
Cape Verde (islands)	Praia	1975 (Portugal)
Gambia	Banjul	1965 (Britain)
Ghana	Accra	1957 (Britain)
Guinea	Conakry	1958 (France)
Guinea-Bissau	Bissau	1974 (Portugal)
Ivory Coast	Yamoussoukro	1960 (France)
Liberia	Monrovia	Independent
Mali	Bamako	1960 (France)
Mauritania	Nouakchott	1960 (France)
Niger	Niamey	1960 (France)
Nigeria	Abuja	1960 (Britain)
Senegal	Dakar	1960 (France)
Sierra Leone	Freetown	1961 (Britain)
Togo	Lomé	1960 (France)
Central Africa		
Cameroon	Yaoundé	1960 (France)
Central African Republic	Bangui	1960 (France)
Chad	N'Djamena	1960 (France)
Congo	Brazzaville	1960 (France)
Equatorial Guinea	Malabo	1968 (Spain)
Gabon	Libreville	1960 (France)
Zaire (Democratic Republic of the Congo, 1997)	Kinshasa	1960 (Belgium)

East Africa

Burundi	Bujumbura	1962 (Belgium)
Comoros (islands)	Moroni	1975 (France)
Djibouti	Djibouti	1977 (France)
Eritrea	Asmara	1993 (Ethiopia)
Ethiopia	Addis Ababa	Independent
Kenya	Nairobi	1963 (Britain)
Madagasgar (island)	Antananarivo	1960 (France)
Rwanda	Kigali	1962 (Belgium)
Somalia	Mogadishu	1960 (Italy, Britain)
Sudan	Khartoum	1956 (Britain, Egypt)
Tanzania	Dodoma	1961 (Britain)
Uganda	Kampala	1962 (Britain)

South Africa

Angola	Luanda	1975 (Portugal)
Botswana	Gaborone	1966 (Britain)
Lesotho	Maseru	1966 (Britain)
Malawi	Lilongwe	1964 (Britain)
Mozambique	Maputo	1975 (Portugal)
Namibia	Windhoek	1990 (South Africa)
South Africa	Pretoria	Independent
Swaziland	Mbabane	1968 (Britain)
Zambia	Lusaka	1964 (Britain)
Zimbabwe	Harare	1980 (Britain)

Geography and Its Influence On African History

Geography is the mother of history because it has influenced the history of many world cultures and civilizations. Africa is no exception to this. Geography still plays an important role in African societies and countries today.

Millions of years ago, the continent of Africa separated from the Asian continent at the Gulf of Suez and the Red Sea, which disconnected northeast Africa from the Arabian peninsula. This was the result

Mt. Kilimanjaro in East Africa

of natural forces that shaped the earth. The earth's outer layer, known as the crust, broke apart and created a deep valley, which stretches from the Red Sea into Ethiopia and down the east coast of Africa to Kenya and Tanzania in the south. This is known as the East African Rift Valley. The African Rift Valley is one of the most beautiful landscapes in the world today. The natural beauty that was created became one of the reasons for European whites settling in East Africa during the early twentieth century.

Geography has made the continent of Africa the cradle of humankind and the place of origin of many civilizations and cultures. The first known African civilization, namely the Egyptian civilization, began along the Nile River. The Nile River is the longest river in the world. It starts at Lake Albert and Victoria and flows northward toward the Mediterranean Sea, where it forms a delta. Other major rivers where African civilizations and empires developed include the Senegal and Niger Rivers in West Africa, the Congo River in Central Africa, and the Zambezi River in southeast Africa.

For a long time, Africa remained isolated from the rest of the world due to oceans, deserts, and forests. Africa is surrounded on all sides by water—the Mediterranean to the north, the Atlantic Ocean to the west, and the Indian Ocean and Red Sea to the east. There are three deserts in Africa, the Sahara Desert in the north and the smaller Kalahari and Namib Deserts in the south. The Sahara Desert (*al-Sahra* in Arabic, which means "desert") occupies the greater part of northern Africa. It was a major barrier separating northern Africa and African territory south of the Sahara, which is known as sub-Saharan Africa. This separation affected the course of African history by keeping the Islamic Civilization in the north largely separated from the African civilizations to the south.

Africa was also rich in natural resources, which included metal ores, precious minerals, and stones, as well as ivory and gold. Metal ores of iron and copper were found scattered throughout the continent. Gold was abundant in West and Central Africa, while diamonds came from South Africa. The Zambezi Valley was known for its sources of gold and ivory. Salt was an important product in North Africa. These resources attracted Europeans to a great extent, resulting in the colonization of the continent in the early twentieth century. Animal life was also abundant in Africa. The Africans regarded the animals as their brothers. In the past, as well as in present times, they depended on the wildlife for their survival as a source of food and trade.

Africa's isolated character and rich resources, as well as its close proximity to water and nature, made it unnecessary for Africans to go beyond their homes. The Africans had everything they needed to survive and live happily. The isolated character of the continent is still apparent today. The European exploitation of African land and human resources has caused Africa to be technologically behind the times. In addition, the problems that African countries faced following their independence has stagnated the economic growth of Africa within the world. This is one reason many of the countries are considered third-world countries today.

The physical landscape in Africa is diverse due in part to the different climates present. There are four types of vegetation in Africa—deserts, woodlands, grasslands, and forests. Tropical rain forest is located around the equator along the south coast of West Africa and into the Congo River basin. North and south of the rain forest, the land changes to woodland and grassland, known as the Savannah. Bordering the Savannah to the north and south lie the deserts. Both the Sahara in the north and the Kalahari and Namib Deserts in the south lie around the 20° lines of latitude. A number of mountain ranges and highlands are scattered throughout North and East Africa, most notably the Atlas Mountains in the north and the Drakensberg Range in the south (see Map 1 on page 83).

Africa can be divided into seven regions:

1. North Africa is the area along the Mediterranean coast from modern Morocco to Libya, including the Sahara Desert. The southern border of this area lies roughly along the 20° north latitude line.

2. Nilotic Africa consists of the lands around the Nile River, in the area of modern Egypt and Sudan.

3. Sudanic Africa is also known as the Sudan region. This area lies below the Sahara Desert, stretching from the Atlantic coast to the Red Sea coastline, from modern Senegal to Ethiopia. (It must be noted that there is some overlap between the Sudan region and West Africa, as well as Nilotic Africa.)

4. West Africa consists of the coastal rain forest region from Cape Verde to Cameroon. This area includes the West Sudanic region, south of the Sahara to Lake Chad.

5. Central Africa lies north of the Kalahari Desert and Zambezi River and east of the Great Rift Valley and Lake Tanganyika.

6. East Africa stretches from Ethiopia along the Great Rift Valley to the Zambezi River.

7. South Africa is the area south of the Zambezi River to the Cape of Good Hope and includes the Kalahari and Namib Deserts.

Name _____ Date _____

Challenges

1. What is the name of the deep valley which lies along the east coast of Africa?

_____

2. What is the longest river in Africa?

_____

3. What is the first known African civilization?

_____

4. Name the five major rivers in Africa.

_____

_____

5. Name the three deserts in Africa.

_____

6. By which bodies of water is Africa surrounded?

_____

_____

7. Africa can be divided into how many regions?

_____

8. Along which latitude lines are the deserts in Africa located?

_____

9. Name the four types of vegetation found in Africa.

_____

_____

10. What natural resources does Africa have?

_____

_____

_____

_____

Name _____ Date _____

Points to Ponder

1. Why were the river basins of Africa good places for the development of many different civilizations?

   _____

   _____

   _____

   _____

   _____

   _____

2. Discuss why Europeans became so involved in the exploration and exploitation of Africa.

   _____

   _____

   _____

   _____

   _____

   _____

Map Activites

1. Using a classroom atlas and the blank map of Africa on page 89, locate and label all of the countries in Africa.

2. Name the seven regions in Africa. Using an atlas and Map 3 on page 85, list the different countries belonging within each region. Color in (with different colors) and label each region on the activity map on page 89.

3. Using Map 2 on page 84 as a reference, draw, color in, and label the four types of vegetation found in Africa on the blank activity map on page 89.

Egyptian Civilization

"Civilization" is defined as an urban society or culture that has developed a complex political institution and social structure, as well as a writing system.

Africa's first and best-known civilization developed along the Nile River in Egypt. For a long time, Egyptian civilization was considered part of the Near Eastern civilizations. However, at least geographically, Egyptian civilization is very much a part of African history and should be included in this survey of Africa. Moreover, Egypt was important because of its relations with the lands to the south on which it had some influence, called Nubia (modern Sudan) and Ethiopia.

As early as 5000 B.C., agriculture, or food production, started in Egypt along the banks of the Nile. Herodotus, a fifth century Greek historian, called Egypt "the gift of the Nile." This shows the importance of the Nile River to Egyptian history and its people. By about 3100 B.C., Egypt had developed into an urban civilization, making it one of the greatest civilizations along the Mediterranean Sea. The rest of Africa at this time was still at the stage of hunting and gathering and, in some places, agriculture. About 3100 B.C., Egypt became united under its first king, called Menes or Narmer. He was the first of a long line of kings to rule Egypt. The last king ruled Egypt until 332 B.C., when it became part of Alexander the Great's empire.

The Egyptians developed a writing system called **hieroglyphics**, which is Greek for "secret writings," because the Greeks could not understand the written symbols used. They also developed an irrigation system to increase their agricultural output and a centralized political system of absolute divine monarchy. The Egyptian king, called a **pharaoh**, had absolute power and was considered a god. To show his power and to guarantee a happy life after death, each pharaoh had great monuments built in his honor. During the Old Kingdom period, these monuments were the pyramids, located near Egypt's capital of Memphis. Memphis was located in the area known as Lower Egypt.

The best-known pyramids of this time period are located on the Gizah plateau. Most notable among the pyramids is the Great Pyramid of the pharaoh Khufu. It is the largest pyramid and, according to Herodotus, took 20 years to build. The pyramid was part of a complex which included a temple, some smaller pyramids called satellite pyramids, and the burial of a life-size ship. The ship was intended to transport the pharaoh into the life beyond. The pharaoh was mummified so that his soul would survive forever, and he was buried in an elaborate wooden coffin decorated with gold, together with all his possessions and provisions of food for his life after death.

The Egyptians belonged to a people who spoke an Afro-Asiatic language. This language group is spread across North Africa. Most anthropologists believe that the Egyptians carried a mixture of physical features from Africa, Asia, and the Mediterranean.

After the Old Kingdom period came a time of chaos known as the First Intermediate period, which was characterized by famine, robbery, and oppression. Egypt was reunified under the kings of Thebes, which starts the Middle Kingdom period. Thebes was located in the area known as Upper Egypt, and the focus of Egyptian civilization moved farther south. The capital was moved to Thebes. It was at this time that the land to the South, Nubia, was added to the Egyptian domain. The pharaohs focused their efforts on trade and agricultural projects to increase agricultural goods.

Another period of civil war and chaos, known as the Second Intermediate period, followed the Middle Kingdom period. Egypt was invaded by an Asiatic Semitic people, called the Hyksos, who ruled Lower Egypt from their capital at Avaris. About 200 years later, the Hyksos were expelled from Egypt by the kings of Thebes, who reunited the land once again. This started a new period known as the New Kingdom period. It was a period of renewed prosperity for Egypt. Not only did Egypt become one of the most powerful civilizations around the Mediterranean between the fifteenth and thirteenth centuries B.C., but it also expanded its territory beyond the Nile into Palestine and Syria and farther south into Nubia. This was accomplished by Pharaoh Tutmosis III. By 1450 B.C., Egyptian civilization extended as far north as Syria and as far south as Nubia. Egyptian prosperity was based on trade throughout the Mediterranean and the Nile River. Most notable among the pharaohs of this period was Ramses II. Ramses II fought many battles against a powerful people in Palestine and Syria, who were expanding their empire into the lands belonging to Egypt. These people were known as the Hittites. One of the most famous battles in history, the battle of Kedesh, occurred around 1270 B.C. It was fought between the Hittites and Ramses II. Both groups claimed their victory, but in fact, it was a Hittite victory, because Egypt lost Syria at this time.

In 1200–1184 B.C., Egypt suffered a major downfall under Ramses III. A group of people, collectively known as the "Sea Peoples," invaded Egypt and brought an end to the prosperity of Egyptian civilization. The following 150 years saw a decline.

The last period in Egyptian history was a period of decadence. This period is called the Post Kingdom period. Egypt was ruled by foreign people from the Near East, the south, and the west continuously until 332 B.C. First came the Lybians in the middle of the tenth century, then came the Nubians in the eighth and seventh centuries. Around 670 B.C., the Semitic Assyrians had created an empire in the Near East that also included Egypt. This was succeeded by the Persian Empire in 526 B.C., and finally Alexander the Great conquered Egypt as part of his empire in 332 B.C.

Following the death of Alexander, the Near East and Egypt were divided among Alexander's generals. Finally one general, Ptolemy, created his new kingdom in 301 B.C. It was named after him—the Ptolemaic Kingdom of Egypt. This lasted until 30 B.C., when Rome conquered Egypt and its last queen, Cleopatra. Egypt then became part of the Roman empire until A.D. 395.

Name _____ Date _____

Challenges

1. Who was responsible for uniting Egypt in 3100 B.C.?

_____

2. What are hieroglyphics?

_____

_____

3. When and where did agriculture develop in Africa?

_____

4. How did Herodotus describe Egypt?

_____

5. What characterized the First and Second Intermediate periods?

_____

_____

6. Who did Ramses II fight in the thirteenth century?

_____

7. Who were the people who invaded Egypt during the Second Intermediate period?

_____

8. Who were the people who invaded Egypt around 1200 B.C. in the reign of Ramses III?

_____

9. In 30 B.C., Egypt was conquered by which empire?

_____

10. Define civilization.

_____

_____

11. Why was Egypt regarded as a civilization?

_____

_____

_____

Name _____ Date _____

Points to Ponder

1. Why is Egypt an important part of the history of Africa?

_____

_____

_____

_____

_____

_____

2. How did the pharaoh show the people that he had divine and absolute power?

_____

_____

_____

_____

_____

_____

3. Compare and contrast the New Kingdom and Post Kingdom periods of Egypt.

_____

_____

_____

_____

_____

_____

North Africa Until the Seventh Century A.D.

By the middle of the second millennium B.C., North Africa up to the Nile valley was inhabited by a people of mixed Saharan origin and Mediterranean stock, known as Berbers. The name Berber is derived from the language that they spoke, not by any particular physical features they possessed. The Berbers were never united into a single group. Rather, they were organized into a number of tribes and led a nomadic way of life. The Berbers were known for the speed and beauty of their horses.

By 1500 B.C., the Berbers were trading with the Egyptians. They probably also traded with the Africans south of the Sahara, although there is no positive evidence of this. During the first millennium B.C., new trading partners, the Phoenicians, appeared on the North African coast.

The Phoenicians came from the coast of the eastern Mediterranean, now modern-day Lebanon. They developed a trade network all over the Mediterranean Sea. Carthage was the most important of their colonies, which they founded between the ninth and fifth centuries B.C. on the coast of North Africa. Other colonies include Leptis and Utica. The Phoenician colonies provided a stimulus for the Berber trade with Sudanic and West Africa. The Berbers became the middlemen between the north to south trade across the Sahara Desert. Trade items traveling northward included gold, ivory, and slaves.

By the third century B.C., the Romans were challenging the Phoenicians in North Africa. By the first century B.C., the Berbers became trading partners with the Romans. Slowly the coast of North Africa came under the control and influence of the Romans. By the first century A.D., many cities, both old and new, flourished along the coast. At this time, trade across the Sahara, called trans-Saharan trade, grew and expanded. Trade grew for two reasons. The Roman cities on the coast served as markets for the Roman trade network. Moreover, the camel was introduced and provided rapid and easy transportation across the Sahara Desert. Again the Berbers acted as intermediaries in the north to south trade across the Sahara.

With the decline and fall of the Roman empire in the fourth and fifth centuries A.D., trade was interrupted. A period of invasions and chaos overwhelmed northern Africa until the seventh century A.D. It was the rise and spread of Islam in this area that led to political stabilization and the revival of the trans-Saharan trade network.

Name _____ Date _____

Challenges

1. Who were the inhabitants of North Africa by the middle of the second millennium B.C.?

_____

2. With whom did the Berbers trade during the first millennium B.C.?

_____

3. Name the most important of Phoenician colonies on the North African coast.

_____

4. What is another term for trade across the Sahara?

_____

5. During Roman times, what were the reasons for the expansion of trade across the Sahara?

_____

_____

_____

6. What trade items were exported from Sudanic and West Africa northwards?

_____

7. What led to the interruption of trade during the fourth and fifth centuries A.D.?

_____

_____

8. What led to the revival of trade across the Sahara in the seventh century A.D.?

_____

_____

Name _____ Date _____

Points to Ponder

1. How did the Berbers adapt to changes in the trading environment in North Africa?

_____

_____

_____

_____

_____

2. Describe the importance of the Mediterranean Sea to the trade system of North Africa.

_____

_____

_____

_____

_____

_____

3. Why does trade break down when governments become unstable?

_____

_____

_____

_____

_____

_____

The Rise and Spread of Islam in North and East Africa

Islam means "to surrender" to the will of the god, Allah; a world religion based on the faith written in the Koran; founded by the prophet Mohammed; adherents to Islam are known as Muslims; fundamental doctrine: "Allah is the only God, and Mohammed is his prophet."

Islam started in the Saudi Arabian peninsula and was founded by the prophet Mohammed (A.D. 571–632). After undergoing a mystical experience in Mecca, Mohammed began to preach and teach his newly acquired faith. Islam was started on

This Islamic mosque in Timbuktu is constructed of mud and wood.

July 16, 622. This date signifies the flight of Mohammed from Mecca to Medina, known as the "Hegira." This date marks the beginning of the Muslim calendar.

After Mohammed's flight to Medina, he became the religious and political leader of his followers. By the time of his death in A.D. 632, Mohammed had united most of the Arabian peninsula under this new faith. The goal of Mohammed's successors was conquest and the conversion to Islam of the entire world. The first phase of expansion happened right after Mohammed's death. During this time (632–661), Islam spread throughout Arabia, Syria, Egypt, Mesopotamia, and east to India, having conquered the Persian Empire. In the next phase (661–750), Muslim expansion went into North Africa, then under Byzantine rule, and from there crossed into Spain. By 750, Islam had reached as far west as Spain and as far east as India.

Islam established political stability and economic recovery throughout the conquered territories, including North Africa, and laid the groundwork for a prosperous civilization. Islamic civilization was a literate, wealthy, and urban civilization. As the Muslims expanded, they assumed local fashion and adapted to local ways. This was one of the reasons why Islamic civilization became so successful.

After 950, political disintegration of the Islamic civilization led to the establishment of several independent political units, such as the Fatimid Dynasty in Egypt, North Africa, Syria, and Arabia (969–1171). The followers of this dynasty became known as Shiites, a sect within the Islam faith. In western North Africa, several Berber Kingdoms arose. The first was the Almoravid Kingdom, followed by the Almohad Kingdom. Despite political disintegration after 950, a major change occurred: Islam superseded Christianity in this area. It was Islamic North Africa that was to greatly influence Africa south of the Sahara.

With the arrival of Islam, the trans-Saharan trade routes were reopened, and new trade routes emerged. Arab Muslim merchants traded far and wide. They established themselves on the coasts of the Indian Ocean, as far as India, China, and East Africa. In North Africa, the Berbers, who had adopted the Islamic faith, once more became the middlemen in the trans-Saharan trade network. The traded goods from Africa grew in demand and included gold, ivory, iron, and slaves.

By the tenth century A.D., networks of commerce had been established far into the interior of the African continent, between North and West Africa, and between East Africa and the central interior. Within the Sudan and along the East African coastline, old markets grew and new markets were founded. These markets turned into prosperous and wealthy cities. Examples of cities in the Sudan include Kumbi, Audagost, Timbuktu, Gao, and Jenne. In East Africa emerged the cities of Kilwa, Zanzibar, Mogadishu, and Mombasa, among many. All these cities flourished and became powerful and wealthy through trade with either the Berbers or the Arabs.

With the trade came also the spread and influence of the Islamic faith and ideals into East and West Africa. However, the degree of influence and Islamic conversion differed between the two regions.

In East Africa, many coastal Africans converted to Islam. Urbanization developed, and the trading markets grew to become prosperous cities. Mosques were built. Intermarriage between the Africans and Arabs also occurred. This helped expand the trading settlements and helped successful trade with the Indian Ocean. This trade was successful until the arrival of the Portuguese in the sixteenth century, when they slowly destroyed what the Africans had built.

The Islam influence in West Africa was more indirect. Islam sought converts primarily in the trading communities within the cities. The townspeople and the people from the countryside never converted to Islam and continued practicing their old traditions. By the thirteenth century, kings of various states also started to convert to the Islamic faith for commercial and political reasons.

From the thirteenth to the sixteenth centuries, Islam expanded into the Sudanic region and helped in the rise of powerful states. Islam brought a literate bureaucracy, Islamic learning, and the idea of centralized power and authority. The influence of Islam was important for two reasons. It revived and expanded commerce, and it helped in the development of powerful states, such as the states of Mali, Songhai, and Kanem-Bornu.

These states acted as middlemen in the trade between the Sudan and the interior along the West African coast. Many powerful small states arose along the coast of West Africa as a result, such as the state of Benin, the Akan states, and the kingdoms of Kongo and Luba. The Africans on the east coast also traded with people from the central interior, creating new political entities in that region, such as the "Great" Zimbabwe Civilization.

20

Name _____ Date _____

Challenges

1. What does Islam mean?

_____

2. Who founded the Islamic religion?

_____

3. What was the Hegira?

_____

4. What was the significance of the Hegira?

_____

_____

5. To what regions in the world did Islam spread within a period of 200 years?

_____

_____

6. What was the reason for the decline of the Islamic civilization in North Africa after A.D. 950?

_____

7. Name three cities in the Sudan region of West Africa that prospered as a result of the reopening of the trans-Saharan trade routes in the eighth century.

_____

8. Name three cities that emerged on the east coast of Africa as a result of the Arab trade with the Indian Ocean.

_____

9. In what two ways did Islam influence sub-Saharan Africa?

_____

_____

10. Name at least three states that were formed south of the Sahara as a result of trade networks and Islamic influence.

_____

_____

Name _____ Date _____

Points to Ponder

1. Describe the rise and expansion of Islam in Africa and Asia.

_____

_____

_____

_____

_____

_____

2. To what extent did Islam spread and influence sub-Saharan Africa?

_____

_____

_____

_____

_____

_____

3. What are the differences between East and West Africa in terms of the degree of Islamic influence?

_____

_____

_____

_____

_____

_____

Sub-Saharan Civilizations: Kush and Axum

South of Egypt, a civilization known as the Kushite civilization emerged in the area of Nubia. The Kushite civilization was divided into two phases, each with a different capital. The Kingdom of Napata flourished between 850 and 600/300 B.C. The Kingdom of Meroe flourished between 600/300 B.C. and A.D. 350.

During the Middle and New Kingdom periods, Egypt conquered Nubia with its two provinces. The north was called Wawat, and the south was called Kush, hence the name Kushite civilization. Both provinces became part of the Egyptian civilization. The origins of the Kushite civilization, which flourished after the decline of the New Kingdom period, lay in a state of which little is known. However, it is the oldest known kingdom in Africa outside of Egypt. This state flourished between 2400–1400 B.C. Its capital was situated at Kerma.

The new Kushite Kingdom had two phases. The first phase was the Kingdom of Napata, with the capital of Napata in the province of Kush. It was rich in gold resources. The wealth gained from trade of these resources gave rise to this new political power. By the eighth century, the Kushites invaded Egypt and ruled most of Egypt for more than 50 years, until 671 B.C. The Kushites established their own

This giant stela at Axum is the only one of seven that still stands.

dynasty of kings in Egypt. The Kushites were expelled from Egypt by a powerful people from the East, called the Assyrians, who brought iron weapons with them. After their expulsion from Egypt, the Kushites became increasingly isolated from Egypt and the rest of the Mediterranean.

The Kingdom of Napata was closely connected to the Egyptian civilization. As a result, it was highly Egyptianized. The Egyptian influence can be seen in their architecture, religion, and use of the Egyptian hieroglyphic script. The Napatan rulers, in fact, saw themselves as Egyptian.

The effects of the introduction of iron by the Assyrians south into Kush marks the beginning of a new powerful phase of the Kushite Civilization. Around 600 B.C., the political and economic center of this civilization started to shift southwards to Meroe. Meroe replaced Napata as the new capital and gave rise to the Kingdom of Meroe. There are several reasons suggested for this shift. Napata was destroyed in 591 B.C. by an Egyptian army.

Other factors may include the desiccation of the region surrounding Napata and the inability to support a growing population. Meroe was better situated for trading with the Red Sea and Ethiopia to the southwest. Meroe was also rich in iron-ore deposits, enabling it to become a center of a flourishing iron industry. Meroe is considered the first known iron-producing center in East Africa.

The Meroitic state of Kush was at its height between the mid-third century B.C. and the third century A.D. Trade with the Mediterranean and the Near East, as well as the production of iron, were major factors in their growth and prosperity. The Meroitic state-system was based on an autocratic centralized rule with an administrative hierarchy in which the ruler and his immediate family were at the head. Although Meroe still had some Egyptian connection, the civilization developed a distinctive culture and broke away from Egyptian influence, unlike their predecessors. The Meroitics borrowed elements of different cultures intermixed with their own and developed their own unique culture. They developed their own alphabetic writing system, worshipped their own deities, and made their own distinctive pottery, and their architectural style was unique. By the second century, Meroe was on a path to decline. Suggested reasons include environmental deterioration, the rise of Axum in the south, and a decline in trade with the north and southwest regions as a result of conflict with the Romans and Axumites. In the fourth century, nomadic incursions and an invasion from Axum brought an end to the Kushite civilization.

To the south of Kush, in northern Ethiopia, emerged a commercially powerful trading state around the first century A.D., the state of Axum. Around A.D. 330, Axum conquered the weakened Meroitic Kingdom of Kush.

The people of Axum were of mixed African origin and Semitic-speaking migrants from southern Arabia. Their chief port was Adulis. Adulis was a major market for ivory and elephants and had become an important commercial center after the Roman conquest of Egypt. Axumite power was due to its strategic location on the Red Sea, which gave access to trade with the Indian Ocean. Moreover, its location was crucial in controlling trade between the interior of Africa and the Roman Empire and southeast Asia. A firm agricultural base was also a factor in its growth. By the third century A.D., Axum was one of the greatest empires in the world. Axum adopted the same state-system as Meroe. It had its own coin mints, striking gold, silver, and copper coins with the kings' names on them. This symbolizes the political and economic power of Axum.

A trademark of the Axumite civilization were the giant towering stelae, up to 33 meters (100 feet) tall and carved like multi-storied buildings. These stelae are considered to be funerary monuments. The height of Axumite power was in the fourth century A.D., when King Ezana conquered Meroe. King Ezana also converted to Christianity, which led to the Christianization of the whole kingdom. The development of the Ethiopian Christian church, in addition to the replacement of Greek by the native Ge'ez language in the fifth century, led eventually to Axum's separation from its Islamic and pagan neighbors, isolating itself culturally from northeast Africa. This lasted until modern times.

Axumite trade with the Mediterranean and the Indian Ocean continued until the sixth century A.D. The state started its decline to obscurity in the seventh to ninth centuries, when the Arabs began to absorb the Red Sea trade.

After Arab Muslim invasions and migrations into Nubia from the thirteenth century onward, which led to the Islamization of Nubia, Ethiopia was left as the sole African Christian state, surrounded by Islam.

Name _____ Date _____

Challenges

1. What are the two phases of the Kushite civilization?

_____

2. Who conquered Meroe in A.D. 330?

_____

3. What brought about the rise of the Kingdom of Napata?

_____

_____

4. What was the chief port city on the Red Sea?

_____

5. What factors led to the rise of the Axumite state?

_____

_____

6. Why did Meroe become the new capital of the second phase of the Kushite civilization?

_____

_____

7. Which Axumite king converted to Christianity?

_____

8. Who drove the Kushite kings out of Egypt in 671 B.C.?

_____

9. What metal ore was introduced in Africa around the seventh century?

_____

10. Who sacked Napata in 591 B.C.?

_____

Name _____ Date _____

Points to Ponder

1. Compare and contrast the Kingdoms of Napata and Meroe.

_____

_____

_____

_____

_____

_____

2. Compare and contrast the decline and fall of Meroe and Axum.

_____

_____

_____

_____

_____

_____

3. What was the significance of King Ezana's conversion to Christianity?

_____

_____

_____

_____

_____

_____

Sub-Saharan Civilizations: The Sudanic Empires

The region south of the Sahara Desert, the Sahel region, was known by Arabs as *bilad al-sudan* or "land of the blacks." Consequently, the term Sudan is used to describe the region south of the Sahara Desert.

In this area, between the eighth and sixteenth centuries A.D., four successive empires rose and fell: Ghana (800–1200), Mali (1100–1700), Songhai (1335–1591), and Kanem-Bornu (1100–1846). These states were also known as the Sudanic empires of western Africa.

There are several reasons for the formation of these states south of the Sahara. Western Africa was rich in valuable resources, such as gold and ivory, which resulted in an accumu-

Sundiata Keita

lation of wealth. External influence from the north in terms of trade and the Islamic religion and ideas also played a major role. After A.D. 750, the expansion of the Muslim trans-Saharan trade provided a stimulus to the western African state formation and urbanization. Finally, the idea of a state may have come from the east of Africa, possibly from Nubia and Ethiopia.

A **state** is a political system with a centralized government, a military force, a civil service, a stratified society, and literacy.

Along the Moroccan-Mauritanian trade routes to North Africa, trading centers were established. Among the cities were Kumbia and Audagost, which were located north of the Upper Niger and Senegal Rivers. Salt from the north was traded for gold and ivory from the south. As a result of this trading system, the Soninke people of Ghana started developing into a state during the eighth century. The capital of the empire of Ghana was established at Kumbi. Ghana reached its height of power during the eleventh century, but soon after, people from the north began to invade the area, most notably the Almoravids, who were Muslims from the north. Finally, people from Takrur in north Senegal seized the Ghana capital, and the empire declined and fell, splitting into different states. Ghana was replaced by the empire of Mali.

One of the states, the chiefdom of Kangaba, inhabited by the Mandinka, formed a new empire under their first king, Sundiata Keita, in 1240. The Kangaba state developed into the empire of Mali with the capital at Niani, another important trading city. Again trade with the north contributed to the growth of the empire, and major towns flourished, among them Timbuktu and Jenne. An additional factor became important in their prosperity: the adoption of Islam. This made Mali a more centralized and literate state than Ghana. The height of the Mali empire was reached around the middle of the fourteenth century, when the empire reached its largest territorial extent, from the Atlantic coast to the borders of

Nigeria and north into the desert. The most famous of the Mali rulers was Mansa Musa (1312–1337). He expanded the empire to its greatest extent. Musa also gave Mali its universal fame when he visited Cairo in 1324, on his way to Mecca on a pilgrimage. In Cairo, he distributed a lot of gold and dressed in great splendor. Musa had adopted Islam, and, as a result, many mosques and a magnificent palace were built. He patronized Muslim scholarship and learning, building several libraries and having several poets at his court. He made the empire of Mali a very wealthy, prosperous, and literate state. However, by 1400, Mali was also on its way to decline.

Tuareg Berbers from the north raided the area, including the city of Timbuktu. Moreover, the growth of another trading city, known as Gao, led to the decline of Mali and the rise of a new and more prosperous state, the Songhai empire. The people of Gao warred against Mali and raided Niani, the capital, in 1400. Finally, in 1464, under Sunni Ali, they conquered their neighbors and developed another empire, also Muslim in nature, called the empire of Songhai.

Sunni Ali (1464–1492) systematically conquered his neighbors, and Songhai became a very powerful state during the fifteenth and sixteenth centuries. Ali fought off a number of raiders, including the Tuareg Berbers from the north and the Mossi from the south. With a strong military, he also took over the cities of Timbuktu and Jenne. This gave him control over an important part of the trade network of the Sudan. Ali also increased and improved upon the central authority of the government, which was organized along the same lines as the Mali empire. He defined provinces for effective administration and created a professional army and navy on the Niger River. Songhai became a more advanced state than that of Mali.

After Ali's death, his successor, Askia Muhammed Turay (1493–1528), continued expanding the empire both east and west, nearly as far west as the Atlantic, as far north as the Sahara, and east into central Sudan. The empire started to decline toward the end of the sixteenth century, however, due to civil war within the empire. Finally, in 1591, an invasion of people from Morocco brought the empire to a close.

The empire of Kanem-Bornu was located around Lake Chad. Unlike the others, Islam was a major influence on the growth and prosperity of this state. Three phases can be distinguished in the history of Kanem-Bornu. The first phase started in the ninth century, when the ruling dynasty, the Sewufa chiefs, gained power in the Lake Chad region. Then, during the eleventh century, with the conversion to Islam, the empire of Kanem, east of Lake Chad, was born due to an increase in trade and the establishment of law and order. This second phase lasted until the fifteenth century, when a rebellion among its subjects brought on a period of confusion. The third phase, which happened at about the same time as the collapse of Songhai, is marked by a shift from the east to the west side of Lake Chad, called Bornu. A new empire emerged and lasted until 1846. It was under Idris Aloona (1575–1610) that the new empire expanded, uniting Kanem and Bornu under a centralized government. Idris Aloona was considered to be the most successful West African monarch of his day.

Name _____ Date _____

Challenges

1. What is a state?

_____

_____

2. Name the four Sudanic empires of West Africa.

_____

_____

3. What was the capital of the empire of Ghana?

_____

4. What led to the downfall of the empire of Ghana?

_____

_____

5. Who founded the empire of Mali?

_____

6. What was the capital of the empire of Mali?

_____

7. How far did the empires of Mali and Songhai extend in territory?

_____

_____

8. What event in 1591 ended the power of the empire of Songhai?

_____

9. Which of the four Sudanic empires lasted the longest?

_____

10. In which area in the Sudan was the empire of Kanem-Bornu located?

_____

Name _____ Date _____

Points to Ponder

1. Compare and contrast the decline and fall of the empires of Ghana, Mali, and Songhai.

_____

_____

_____

_____

_____

_____

2. Describe the different factors that led to the formation of states in the Sudan.

_____

_____

_____

_____

_____

_____

Map Activity

Using Map 4 on page 86 as a resource, outline and color the extent of each of the four Sudanic states in West Africa on the blank activity map on page 89.

Sub-Saharan Civilizations: Kingdoms and States South of the Sudan

Civilizations also rose along the west coast of Africa and its interior. Kingdoms and states developed around A.D. 1000 and had become prosperous and powerful by the time the Portuguese landed on the coast of Africa during the fifteenth century. These new states were located along the mouth of the Senegal, Niger, and Congo Rivers. The states of Benin and Yoruba developed along the Niger River. The Kingdoms of Kongo and Luba were founded along the Congo River.

One of the factors that led to the rise of states south of the Sudan was the spread of the idea of "divine kingship." This concept was common to the Sudanic states, and it moved southward in association with new people from the north. Other factors include the growth of trade and production for trade. Producing items specifically for trade was made possible by the fertility of the land and the abundance of metal resources from the environment. The people of these states practiced intensive agriculture and became craftsmen in metallurgy.

These bronze figures are of a Benin warrior and his attendant.

The states of Benin and Yoruba were organized in a different way from the Sudanic empires of Ghana, Mali, and Songhai. Benin and Yoruba consisted of a loose confederation of city-states, with only one of the city-states becoming powerful enough to control the others. Trade was a major factor in their rise to power. In fact, the people within these states were intermediaries in the north-to-south trade system. The kings of both states strengthened their power and control by reducing the power of the nobility and instead creating "town-chiefs" loyal to the king and under his king. The appointment of these "town-chiefs" was based on their wealth achieved by farming, trade, and warfare, rather than through hereditary rights. Both Benin and Yoruba states were based on a hierarchy of chiefs rather than the one ruler. The monarch, however, was the absolute and most powerful ruler at the top of the pyramid. He controlled the affairs of the state, including trade and rituals. The kings of Benin and Yoruba had thus increased the centralization of their governments.

By 1500, the Portuguese had landed on this coast and found very powerful and wealthy states, with whom they started trading. The West Africans traded pepper, gold, ivory, and slaves in return for glass beads, cloth, and eventually weapons.

Two other kingdoms in Southwest Africa, the Kingdoms of Luba and Kongo, were formed south of Benin and Yoruba along the Congo River. Agriculture had developed south of the equator by A.D. 800. It was the Kongolo people, who practiced intensive agriculture, who formed the Luba Kingdom (1000–1600). Individuals who were leaders of their own kinship groups assumed economic and political power through the wealth acquired from the land. These leaders united several villages and developed a state. The Luba Kingdom was ruled by a feudal system—a hierarchical system with the king at the top, delegating authority to the level of leaders below. In turn, the second-level leaders delegated authority to a third level of leaders below them.

The Kingdom of Kongo (1200–1600) rose slowly on the coast of Southwest Africa. It is the most famous of all the kingdoms south of the Sudan because of the numerous written sources describing the kingdom. The Kongo Kingdom was a Sudanic-type state, where the king was the absolute monarch and was considered divine. After expanding his territory and incorporating smaller states, the king ruled over a series of provinces, each ruled by governors. Trade was controlled by the king. He lived in the capital city, Mbanza, which served several functions. The capital was a fortress, and the king's court was located within it. It was also a trading center between the coast and the interior, and it served as a religious center.

The Kongo Kingdom was the first African kingdom to be visited by the Portuguese in 1483. The Portuguese traded with the Africans, demanding primarily slaves. At first, the relations were diplomatic and peaceful, but they soon turned ugly and led to the downfall of the Kongo Kingdom. The most famous Kongo king was Alfonso I (1506–1543), who wrote a number of letters to the Portuguese government, complaining of the effects of enslaving the Kongo people. He was also the first to accept the new religion of Christianity. It shows the dual nature of the Portuguese's interest in Africa—slaves and the conversion of the Africans to Christianity.

King Alfonso of Kongo writes the following letter to the Portuguese monarch in 1526 (abstract from a letter, in Basil Davidson, *The African Past*, New York, 1967, p. 191–193).

"Sir, Your Highness should know how our Kingdom is being lost in so many ways that it is convenient to provide for the necessary remedy, since this is caused by the excessive freedom given by your factors and officials to the men and merchants who are allowed to come to this Kingdom to set up shops with goods and many things which have been prohibited by us, and which they spread throughout our Kingdoms and Domains in such an abundance that many of our vassals, whom we had in obedience, do not comply...it is doing a great harm not only to the service of God, but the security and peace of our Kingdom and State as well. And we cannot reckon how great the damage is, since the mentioned merchants are taking every day our natives...they grab them and get them to be sold; and so great, Sir, is the corruption and licentiousness that our country is being completely depopulated...That is why we beg of Your Highness to help and assist us in this matter, commanding your factors that they should not send here either merchants or wares, because it is our will that in these Kingdoms there should not be any trade of slaves nor outlet for them."

Name _____ Date _____

Challenges

1. Name the four states that developed south of the Sudan around A.D. 1000.

_____

_____

2. Along which river did the states of Benin and Yoruba develop?

_____

3. Along which river did the states of Kongo and Luba develop?

_____

4. Who were the first Europeans to land on the coast of West Africa?

_____

5. For what commodities did the Europeans want to trade with the Africans?

_____

_____

6. What did the Africans receive in return?

_____

_____

7. Which of the four African kingdoms south of the Sudan do we know the most about?

_____

8. Who was the most famous king of Kongo who converted to Christianity?

_____

9. What did this king complain about in his letters to the Portuguese monarch?

_____

_____

10. What was the capital of the Kongo Kingdom?

_____

Name _____ Date _____

Points to Ponder

1. Compare and contrast the states of Benin and Kongo.

_____

_____

_____

_____

_____

2. What were the factors that led to the rise of the states south of the Sudan?

_____

_____

_____

_____

_____

3. What two major points were made by King Alfonso in his letter to the Portuguese monarch in 1526? Pretend you are the Portuguese monarch and write a letter in return, indicating the points you would make to defend your actions in Kongo.

_____

_____

_____

_____

_____

Map Activity

Using Map 4 on page 86 as a resource, outline and color the extent of the four states south of the Sudan on the blank activity map on page 89.

Sub-Saharan Civilizations: East Africa, A.D. 1000–1600

The ruins of "Great Zimbabwe"

In East Africa between A.D. 1000 and 1600, powerful coastal city-states emerged. These were located between what is today Somalia and Mozambique. These city-states grew as a result of trade contacts with South Asia and Arabia. Arabs, Persians, Indians, and Malaysians are said to have visited the east coast for commercial pursuits. Africans exported goods such as ivory, incense, spices, gold, iron, slaves, and perfumed oils in return for glazed pottery, cloth, glass beads, and china. With the wealth acquired through trade, the Africans built cities as centers of trade. These cities became self-governing; therefore, they were called city-states. Because of Arab influence, Islam became the dominant religion in these cities, and numerous mosques were built. Examples of these city-states were Kilwa, Mombasa, Zanzibar, and Mogadishu. An urban culture had developed along the coast of East Africa.

A culture known as Swahili developed between 1200 and 1400 in this area, combining the African and Islamic features. To facilitate trade and communication between the Arab-speaking merchants and Bantu-speaking Africans, a common language developed called Swahili (from the Arabic *sawahil,* meaning "coastlands"). The height of the Swahili culture came during the fourteenth and fifteenth centuries.

Ruling dynasties governed these cities. The rulers were known as sultans. The society consisted of the local nobility, commoners, resident foreigners employed in the local commerce, and slaves.

These ports of trade were visited in the early sixteenth century by the Portuguese. This eventually led to their decline and downfall. During the seventeenth century, the Portuguese conquered and destroyed many of the East African city-states.

At the same time as these cities were flourishing, another civilization occupied the area between the Limpopo and Zambezi Rivers—the civilization of Zimbabwe. This civilization was purely African with no Islamic influences. It was founded about 1150 and centered on a major city, "Great Zimbabwe," which was probably the capital. This city was thought to have been built by the ancestors of the Shona people who live in the area today. Zimbabwe became a very wealthy and prosperous state for a variety of reasons: the control of the gold resources in the area, intensive agriculture, and trade with the coastal city-states.

Before the arrival of the Portuguese in the sixteenth century, Zimbabwe collapsed for reasons unknown. The most accepted theory is the collapse and exhaustion of farming in the area, leading to the abandonment of the city.

Name _____ Date _____

Challenges

1. What is a city-state?

_____

_____

2. Who was involved in the Indian Ocean trade along the east coast of Africa?

_____

3. What commodities did the Africans export?

_____

_____

4. What commodities did the Africans import?

_____

_____

5. Who were the first Europeans to visit the east coast of Africa?

_____

6. What culture developed in East Africa by 1400?

_____

7. Name some of the city-states that grew prosperous as a result of the Indian Ocean trade.

_____

_____

8. Between which rivers did the Zimbabwe civilization develop?

_____

9. What factors led to the rise of the Zimbabwe civilization?

_____

_____

10. Why did the Zimbabwe civilization collapse?

_____

_____

Name _____ Date _____

Points to Ponder

1. Describe and give examples of the different types of state-systems that developed throughout sub-Saharan Africa prior to 1600.

_____

_____

_____

_____

_____

_____

2. To what extent did Islam contribute to the development of states throughout sub-Saharan Africa prior to the arrival of the Europeans?

_____

_____

_____

_____

_____

_____

Map Activity

1. Using Map 4 on page 86 as a resource, outline and color the extent of the Zimbabwe civilization on the blank activity map on page 89.

2. Locate and label the following city-states on the activity map: Kilwa, Mombasa, Zanzibar, and Mogadishu.

The Atlantic Slave Trade, Part 1

European contact during the latter part of the fifteenth century along the West African coast resulted in significant changes in sub-Saharan Africa starting about 1500. The most significant change was the beginning of the Atlantic slave trade, which affected the African people by changing their lifestyles in many ways.

Prior to 1500, the West Africans had faced an empty ocean; the Africans had not built ships and had not sailed across the ocean. They were content remaining on their continent, toiling their land, and hunting game. This changed, however, when the Portuguese started to sail along the West African coast. The Portuguese started to trade with the West Africans along the coast. They traded with several chiefdoms and states along the Guinea coast, most notably with the Wolof state at the mouth of the Senegal River, with the Akan states of the central region, as well as with chiefdoms and states along the Niger and Congo Rivers, such as Benin and the Kongo empire. Trade consisted of exchanging gold, ivory, and a small number of slaves. Slave trade was minor during that time. At first, the Portuguese formed trading partnerships with the West Africans, and the trade relations were friendly. But the discovery of the Americas was to change this relationship.

The Americas, most specifically Central and South America, were discovered in the 1400s by the Spanish and Portuguese. The Spanish and Portuguese began to operate large plantations and mines in these newly-discovered regions with the use of the native people as slave labor. However, the native Indians were not used to hard labor like the Europeans wanted, and they started dying in alarming numbers. Eventually there were not many natives left to work the plantations and the mines. The Spanish and Portuguese found what seemed to be the perfect solution in about 1500 in Africa.

In 1510, the sale of Africans in the Americas was legalized by the Spanish crown. In 1518, the first cargo of Africans sailed in a Spanish ship from Guinea to America. So began the West Atlantic Slave Trade. It was to last two and a half centuries, and about 10 to 12 million Africans were carried across—about two million Africans died on the way. The slave trade was to become disastrous for the Africans.

The question to ask now is: Why Africa? Why did it happen so easily? First, slave trade was not uncommon and strange within Africa. For centuries, slaves were traded with the Muslims of North and East Africa. Slaves were usually prisoners of war or those people punished for a crime. They were seen and used like servile people. They were used in the household or military services. However, the African economy was not a slave-based economy. The slaves were like wageless workers, and if they wanted, they could work for themselves, free from obligations. In short, the African slaves were more like serfs. Hence, trading in slaves was neither uncommon nor strange for the Africans. In fact, the early sale of African slaves did not depart drastically from the previous practices of the Africans themselves. The only difference was the transportation of slaves across the ocean.

Second, the Africans were many, and they were skilled farmers and miners, hence they were very valuable as labor, not only for the Europeans but also for the Africans. When the European demand for slaves rose in the seventeenth and eighteenth centuries, this trade dealt purely with captives of war. As a result, different African coastal federations rose who joined hands with the European merchants in exploiting their own people and acted as middlemen in the slave trade. These Africans did not realize the negative consequences of their actions; they were thinking of the short-term profit from the sale of the slaves. To procure and capture the slaves for the Europeans, these African federations would make war on their neighbors. In return, European goods were exchanged, such as firearms, tobacco, alcohol, and cotton. The slave trade could only survive through warfare and violence. The Africans were caught up in a vicious circle: the need for captives for the Europeans increased the need for firearms, and the increased availability of firearms increased warfare and violence among the African nations.

The high point of slavery occurred between 1650 and 1850. Slavery was inhumane. The slaves were treated like cattle, and tests were done on them to ensure their strength. On their journey to the Americas, the slaves were crammed and chained below the decks. Then the slaving ship would proceed slowly across the ocean, hoping only 10 to 15 percent of the cargo of slaves would die.

The Portuguese were the principal carriers of the slave trade until the 1640s, when the Dutch, French, and British entered the trade.

Indigenous African slavery began to decline at the end of the nineteenth century, beginning in 1874 and ending in 1928. This was partly as a result of British and French abolitionists fighting to make an end to slavery. Also, by this time, European interests were changing and demand for slave labor diminished. The Europeans now went in search of raw materials, prestige, and military gain as the Industrial Revolution swept through Europe.

Slave Exports from Africa (from Robert July, *A History of the African People*, 5th ed., 1998, p. 173):

period	volume
1450–1600	367,000
1601–1700	1,868,000
1701–1800	6,133,000
1801–1900	3,330,000
Total	11,698,000

Personal account describing the Atlantic passage:

Olaudah Equiano

The first object which saluted my eyes when I arrived on the coast was the sea, a slaveship, which was then riding at anchor, and waiting for its cargo. These filled me with astonishment, which was soon converted to terror, which I am yet at a loss to describe, nor the then feelings of my mind. When I was carried on board I was immediately handled, and tossed up, to see if I were sound, by some of the crew; and I was now persuaded that I had got into a world of bad spirits, and that they were going to kill me. Their complexions too differing so much from ours, their long hair, and the language they spoke, which was very different from any I had ever heard, united to confirm me in this belief. Indeed, such were the horrors of my views and fears at the moment, that, if ten thousand worlds had been my own, I would have freely parted with them all to have exchanged my condition with that of the meanest slave in my own country. When I looked round the ship too, and saw a large furnace or copper boiling, and a multitude of black people of every description chained together, every one of their countenances expressing dejection and sorrow, I no longer doubted my fate; and, quite overpowered with horror and anguish, I fell motionless on the deck and fainted. When I recovered a little, I found some black people about me, who I believed were some of those who brought me on board, and had been receiving their pay; they talked to me in order to cheer me, but all in vain. I asked them if we were not to be eaten by those white men with horrible looks, red faces, and long hair. They told me I was not; and one of the crew brought me a small portion of spirituous liquor in a wine-glass; but, being afraid of him, I would not take it out of his hand. One of the blacks therefore took it from him, and gave it to me, and I took a little down my palate, which, instead of reviving me, as they thought it would, threw me into the greatest consternation at the strange feeling it produced having never tasted any such liquor before. Soon after this, the blacks who brought me on board went off, and left me abandoned to despair. I now saw myself deprived of all chance of returning to my native country, or even the least glimpse of hope of gaining the shore, which I now considered as friendly; and I even wished for my former slavery, in preference to my present situation, which was filled with horrors of every kind, still heightened by my ignorance of what I was to undergo. I was not long suffered to indulge my grief; I was soon put down under the decks, and there I received such a salutation in my nostrils as I had never experienced in my life; so that, with the loathsomeness of the stench, and crying together, I became so sick and low that I was not able to eat, nor had I the least desire to taste any thing. I now wished for the last friend, death, to relieve me; but soon, to my grief, two of the white men offered me eatables; and, on my refusing to eat, one of them held me fast by the hands, and laid me across, I think, the windlass, and tied my feet while the other flogged me severely. I had never experienced any thing of this kind before; and, although not being used to the water, I naturally feared that element the first time I saw it; yet, nevertheless, could

I have got over the nettings, I would have jumped over the side; but I could not; and, besides, the crew used to watch us very closely who were not chained down to the decks, lest we should leap into the water: and I have seen some of these poor African prisoners most severely cut for attempting to do so, and hourly whipped for not eating. This indeed was often the case with myself. In a little time after, amongst the poor chained men, I found some of my own nation, which in a small degree gave ease to my mind. I inquired of them what was to be done of us? they gave me to understand we were to be carried to these white people's country to work for them. I then was a little revived, and thought, if it were no worse than working, my situation was not so desperate: but still I feared I should be put to death, the white people looked and acted, as I thought, in so savage a manner; for I had never seen among any people such instances of brutal cruelty; and this not only shown towards us blacks, but also to some of the whites themselves. One white man in particular I saw, when we were permitted to be on deck, flogged so unmercifully with a large rope near the foremast, that he died in consequence of it; and they tossed him over the side as they would have done a brute. This made me fear these people the more; and I expected nothing less than to be treated in the same manner. I could not help expressing my fears and apprehensions to some of my countrymen: I asked them if these people had no country, but lived in this hollow place the ship? they told me they did not, but came from a distant one. "Then," said I, "how comes it in all our country we never heard of them?" They told me, because they lived so very far off. I then asked, where were their women? had they any like themselves? I was told they had. "And why," said I, "do we not see them?" they answered, because they were left behind. I asked how the vessel could go? they told me they could not tell; but that there were cloth put upon the masts by the help of the ropes I saw, and then the vessel went on; and the white men had some spell or magic they put in the water when they liked in order to stop the vessel. I was exceedingly amazed at this account, and really thought they were spirits. I therefore wished much to be from amongst them, for I expected they would sacrifice me: but my wishes were vain; for we were so quartered that it was impossible for any of us to make our escape. While we staid on the coast I was mostly on

deck; and one day, to my great astonishment, I saw one of these vessels coming in with the sails up. As soon as the whites saw it, they gave a great shout, at which we were amazed: and the more so as the vessel appeared larger by approaching nearer. At last she came to an anchor in my sight, and when the anchor was let go, I and my countrymen who saw it were lost in astonishment to observe the vessel and stop; and were now convinced it was done by magic. Soon after this the other ship got her boats out, and they came on board of us, and the people of both ships seemed very glad to see each other. Several of the strangers also

Slaves were packed onto ships as tightly as possible for the journey from Africa to the New World.

shook hands with us black people, and made motions with their hands, signifying, I suppose, we were to go to their country; but we did not understand them. At last, when the ship we were in had got in all her cargo, they made ready with many fretful noises, and we were all put under deck, so that we could not see how they managed the vessel. But this disappointment was the least of my sorrow. The stench of the hold while we were on the coast was so intolerably loathsome, that it was dangerous to remain there for any time, and some of us had been permitted to stay on the deck for the fresh air; but now that the whole ship's cargo were confined together, it became absolutely pestilential. The closeness of the place, and the heat of the climate, added to the number in the ship, which was so crowded that each had scarcely room to turn himself, almost suffocated us. This produced copious perspirations, so that the air soon became unfit for respiration, from a variety of loathsome smells, and brought on a sickness amongst the slaves, of which many died, thus falling victims to the improvident avarice, as I may call it, of their purchasers. This wretched situation was again aggravated by the galling of the chains, now become insupportable; and the filth of the necessary tubs, into which the children often fell, and were almost suffocated. The shrieks of the women, and the groans of the dying, rendered the whole a scene of horror almost inconceivable. Happily perhaps for myself I was soon reduced so low here that it was thought necessary to keep me almost always on deck; and from my extreme youth I was not put in fetters. In this situation I expected every hour to share the fate of my companions, some of whom were almost daily brought upon deck at the point of death, which I began to hope would soon put an end to my miseries. Often did I think many of the inhabitants of the deep much more happy then myself; I envied them the freedom they enjoyed, and as often wished I could change my condition for theirs. Every circumstance I met with served only to render my state more painful, and heighten my apprehensions and my opinion of the cruelty of the whites...

At last, we came in sight of the island of Barbadoes, at which the whites on board gave a great shout, and made many signs of joy to us. We did not know what to think of this; but, as the vessel drew nearer, we plainly saw the harbour, and other ships of different kinds and sizes: and we soon anchored amongst them off Bridge Town. Many merchants and planters now come on board, though it was in the evening. They put us in separate parcels, and examined us attentively. They also made us jump, and pointed to the land, signifying we were to go there. We thought by this we should be eaten by these ugly men, as they appeared to us; and when, soon after we were all put down under the deck again, there was much dread and trembling among us, and nothing but bitter cries to be heard all the night from these apprehensions, insomuch that at last the white people got some old slaves from the land to pacify us. They told us we were not to be eaten, but to work, and were soon to go on land where we should see many of our country people. This report eased us much; and sure enough, soon after we landed, there came to us Africans of all languages. We were conducted immediately to the merchant's yard, where we were all pent up together like so many sheep in a fold, without regard to sex or age. As every object was new to me, everything I saw filled me with surprise. What struck me first was, that the houses were built with bricks, in stories, and in every other respect different from those I have seen in Africa: but I was still more astonished on seeing people on horseback. I did not know what this could mean; and indeed I thought these people were full of nothing but magical arts. While I was in this astonishment, one of my fellow prisoners spoke to a countryman of his about the horses, who said they were the same kind they had in their country. I understood them, though they were from a distant part of Africa, and I thought it odd I had not seen any horses there; but afterwards, when I came to converse with different Africans, I found they had many horses amongst them, and much larger than those I then saw. We were not many days in the merchant's custody, before we were sold after their usual manner, which is this: on a signal given (as the beat of a drum), the buyers rush at once into the yard where the slaves are confined, and make choice of the parcel they like best. The noise and clamour with which this is attended, and the eagerness visible in the countenances of the buyers, serve not a little to increase the apprehension of the terrified Africans, who may well be supposed to consider them as the ministers of that destruction to which they think themselves devoted. In this manner, without scruple, are relations and friends separated, most of them never to see each other again. I remember in the vessel in which I was brought over, in the men's apartment, there were several brothers who, in the sale, were sold in different lots; and it was very moving on this occasion to see and hear their cries at parting. O, ye nominal Christians! might not an African ask you, learned you this from your God? who says unto you, Do unto all men as you would men should do unto you. Is it not enough that we are torn from our country and friends to toil for your luxury and lust of gain? Must every tender feeling be likewise sacrificed to your avarice? Are the dearest friends and relations, now rendered more dear by their separation from their kindred, still to be parted from each other, and thus preventing from cheering the gloom of slavery with the small comfort of being together, and mingling their sufferings and sorrows? Why are parents to love their children, brothers their sisters, or husbands their wives? Surely this is a new refinement in cruelty, which, while it has no advantage to atone for it, thus aggravates distress, and adds fresh horrors even to the wretchedness of slavery.

from *The Interesting Narrative of the life of Olaudah Equiano; or, Gustavus Vasa, the African* (2 vols., London, 1789, abstracts from Ch. 2., p. 44–57).

Name _____ Date _____

Challenges

1. What was the Atlantic Slave Trade?

_____

_____

2. What event brought on the beginning of the Atlantic Slave Trade?

_____

3. How many Africans were exported to the Americas between the fifteenth and early twentieth centuries?

_____

4. Which century experienced the largest export of slaves from Africa?

_____

5. Who were the primary carriers throughout the history of the slave trade?

_____

6. Was the Atlantic Slave Trade the first of any kind of slave trade occurring in Africa? If not, where did slave trade occur?

_____

_____

7. How were some Africans involved in the slave trade?

_____

_____

8. What goods did the Europeans exchange for slaves?

_____

9. Between which two dates did the Atlantic Slave Trade thrive?

_____

10. What were the reasons that brought the slave trade to an end by the early twentieth century?

_____

_____

_____

Name _____ Date _____

Points to Ponder

1. Why did the Portuguese look for slaves in Africa? Why was Africa such an easy target?

_____

_____

_____

_____

_____

_____

2. Why did the Portuguese and Spanish need slaves by 1500?

_____

_____

_____

_____

_____

_____

3. Read the account on pages 40–43. Describe the conditions of slaves while sailing across the Atlantic.

_____

_____

_____

_____

_____

_____

The Atlantic Slave Trade, Part 2

The transatlantic slave trade had several consequences for Africans. However, the extent to which the trade affected the Africans is a much-debated topic, partially due to the lack of concrete evidence and partially due to the differences in the state of affairs among African societies.

African middlemen often captured slaves in the interior of the continent and marched them to the coast to be sold.

One of the effects the trade had on Africa was the degradation of the Africans and the beginning of racism. Ideas of European "racial superiority," which took root in the nineteenth and twentieth centuries, eventually led to the occupation of Africa by several European powers.

One of the most commonly cited consequences was the depopulation among the Africans, especially the strong, young males. But the evidence shows regional differences of the effects of the slave trade. The states of Benin and Yoruba were affected little by the trade, while the areas along the Slave Coast yielded moderate amounts of population loss, and the Kongo-Angola region witnessed major depopulation. Despite these specific examples, the slave trade did not have an influential impact on African society as a whole, with respect to depopulation. Accurate information on estimates of the African population during the four centuries is lacking. It is also not known exactly how many of the slaves were captured as a result of slave raids or local wars. Furthermore, the export of 11.5 million slaves to the Americas was spread over 400 years and extended over vast areas. The impact of the European slave trade on Africa was minimal compared to the impact of European colonialism in the twentieth century.

The slave trade was also economically and politically destructive for some areas in West Africa. The trade in slaves was replaced by trade in cheap industrial goods, which led Africa to become dependent on European goods rather than producing their own goods. It undermined the local production of cotton and metal goods and discouraged expansion. It also deprived many African societies of their producers. In fact, capitalism was not to develop in Africa until the end of the nineteenth century, and when it did, colonialism put a stop to it.

While the slave trade did destroy many societies in the near-coastal areas, further inland some Africans gained from the trade. Small states began to take shape while others prospered. The Yoruba Kingdom grew in size and strength during the eighteenth century. A new empire, the Asanti empire, rose in central and coastal Ghana. By the nineteenth century, a number of West African societies along the Niger Delta were producing their own palm oil instead of slaves. They had their own plantations, but they did not have industrial production. However, their efforts were dampened by European colonialism.

Name _____ Date _____

Challenges

1. Which people felt they were "racially superior" to the Africans?

_____

2. Which members of the African population were especially decreased by the slave trade?

_____

3. What region of Africa experienced major depopulation?

_____

4. For how many years were slaves exported to the Americas?

_____

5. What type of trade was conducted after the slave trade stopped?

_____

_____

6. What goods were being produced in Africa before European colonization?

_____

_____

7. Name two empires that prospered during the slave trade years.

_____

8. Where was palm oil being produced?

_____

_____

Name _____ Date _____

Points to Ponder

1. List and describe the effects of the transatlantic slave trade on West Africa.

_____

_____

_____

_____

_____

_____

2. To what extent were the consequences of the slave trade negative?

_____

_____

_____

_____

_____

_____

_____

3. To what extent were the consequences of the slave trade positive?

_____

_____

_____

_____

_____

_____

_____

Sudan and East Africa During the Eighteenth and Nineteenth Centuries

Slave dealers inspect a slave in Zanzibar.

Further inland in the Sudan region, slave trade had no influence on the political developments of the eighteenth and nineteenth centuries. After the fall of Songhai in 1591, the Sudan region entered a period of rebellions and invasions from the north and south. From this chaos, a new political pattern emerged, due to the revival of Islam. Islam was reviving its power in the form of militant and reform movements of *jihad* (meaning "holy struggle"). Islam tried to make a lasting mark on West Africa. States were established by incoming settlers, most notably the Fulani. They were pastoralists who had converted to the Islamic faith. The most important of these Islamic reform movements was led by a Fulani scholar, Usman Dan Fodio (1754–1817). He led the Fulani in the conquest of the Hausa territory in north central Nigeria and brought Islam into this area. Not only the rulers, but the whole countryside converted to Islam. Muslim schools of learning and mosques were built throughout this area. Usman Dan Fodio's son, Muhammed Bello, expanded his father's power and built his capital at Sokoto, establishing the Sokoto empire.

In East Africa, a different picture emerged during the eighteenth and nineteenth centuries. During the seventeenth century, the Portuguese had destroyed the trade system with nations of the Indian Ocean, and Africans lost many of the coastal settlements they had established. The Africans allied themselves with the Arabs from Oman, in Saudi Arabia, who helped them expel the Portuguese. The Portuguese were left with the southern coastal area of East Africa. During the eighteenth and nineteenth centuries, the Arab Muslims slowly rebuilt the Indian Ocean trade system with the help of the local Africans. Swahili culture slowly recovered. Slave trading and raiding became an important part of the commerce with the Arabs on the central-north part of the coast. The French and Portuguese were trading slaves heavily on the southern part of the coast. Slaves were obtained from the interior of Africa, and this created disruption and increased local warfare in the interior until the arrival of colonialism.

The late eighteenth and nineteenth centuries were also the time of European explorations in the Africa interior. The purpose was not conquest or commerce, but rather to know and understand the shape and layout of the African continent in the pursuit of science. Explorers such as Mungo Park in Western Sudan and David Livingstone in East and Central Africa are two examples. Philanthropists sought to "civilize the Africans" and to introduce Christianity. Christian mission schools were set up with the goal to convert and educate the Africans.

Name _____ Date _____

Challenges

1. What is a *jihad*?

_____

2. Who led the Islamic reform movement into the Hausa territory of northern Nigeria in the eighteenth century?

_____

3. Who established the Sokoto empire?

_____

4. Who were the Fulani?

_____

_____

5. Who was responsible for the destruction of the Indian Ocean trade in the seventeenth century?

_____

6. Who rebuilt the Indian Ocean trade system during the eighteenth and nineteenth centuries?

_____

7. Name two European explorers of Africa.

_____

8. Why was the Sudan an area of chaos during the sixteenth and seventeenth centuries?

_____

_____

9. What was the purpose for European exploration of inner Africa?

_____

_____

10. What were the consequences of the east coast African slave trade on the interior of central-east Africa?

_____

_____

Name _____ Date _____

Points to Ponder

1. How was the introduction of Islam responsible for a more stable political environment in the Sudan?

_____

_____

_____

_____

_____

_____

_____

_____

_____

_____

_____

2. Discuss reasons why philanthropists and missionaries did not recognize the legitimacy of African civilization.

_____

_____

_____

_____

_____

_____

_____

_____

_____

_____

_____

Imperialism and Colonialism in Africa, Part 1, 1880–1914

Imperialism—the exercise of power by a state beyond its boundaries
Colonialism—a form of imperialism; the administrative control by a state over other people

This political cartoon depicts the Imperialistic view that Europeans could easily dominate Africa.

The transatlantic slave trade helped Europe in starting the Industrial Revolution. Slaving was part of the massive overseas trade, which brought money to European economic development and brought Europe into world dominance. Europe became so dominant that it was able to colonize Africa in the late nineteenth/early twentieth century.

European imperialism and colonization in Africa can be divided into two phases. Phase I constituted the actual conquest and partition of Africa by the European powers. The largest of these powers were France and Britain, controlling about two-thirds of the African continent. The other major European powers who contended for African territory were Belgium, Germany, Italy, Portugal, and Spain. This phase is also known as "the scramble for Africa." Phase II consisted of the actual control over the African people. The establishment of a system of political and economic control was known as colonialism. For Africa and the Africans, this period in their history is a continuation of the slave trade period, because the Europeans once again exploited the African people. It was, however, a different type of exploitation. The Europeans not only took away their land, but they also employed them as cheap labor in the exploitation of their own natural resources, all of which benefited the European countries, rather than the Africans themselves.

There were three reasons for Europeans to explore the African continent, which eventually led to the colonization of Africa: scientific interest, the spread of Christianity, and imperialism. The nineteenth century in Europe was an age of curiosity for unknown lands, in particular Asia and Africa.

The late eighteenth and nineteenth centuries also brought about the rise of a new belief, called **ethnocentrism**, among the European people. It is a belief whereby one group of people feels superior to other groups of people, due primarily to cultural differences. This belief was prevalent among the Europeans who believed that the Africans were inferior and "uncivilized," because they were not technologically advanced and still lived in "primitive" ways. It was their duty to "civilize" the Africans, and hence they felt it their right to take over Africa. This belief goes hand-in-hand with the idea of spreading Christianity throughout

Africa and converting the Africans in the process. This process of Christianization of the Africans was, in fact, part of the European ideology of "civilizing" them. The Christian missionaries set up schools and churches, teaching them the English language and Christian ways.

The third motivating factor was imperialism. Imperialism took on many forms, in terms of political, economic, and cultural claims. Politically, the European powers wanted power and prestige. Wealth in terms of territorial gains meant power, and the more territory a country controlled, the more powerful it was. Territorial control was also advantageous during wars. It gave the country geopolitical or strategic advantages elsewhere in the world. During the nineteenth century, the British and the French patrolled the coastlines as part of the anti-slavery movements. They appointed consuls who gained influence among the African communities. Economically, Africa was rich in resources and cheap labor. Merchant-adventurers were drawn to the riches of Africa and could attain personal wealth and prestige. The cultural aspect of imperialism has to do, once again, with the ethnocentric view of the European people. The Europeans felt it was their duty to "civilize" the Africans.

Consequently, the traders, the missionaries, and the consuls gained and extended imperial influence along the coastal communities in Africa, in the name of trading goods, in the name of security and protection, and in the name of God. The merchant-adventurers urged their respective governments to secure colonies that would serve as sources for raw materials and markets for manufactured goods. The European leaders started responding more positively by the 1880s, leading to the "scramble for Africa." The Africans themselves were so dependent on the Europeans for overseas trade that they had not thought to create a resistance, nor did they know of the consequences it might create.

International rivalry between the French and the British heralded the scramble in West Africa for the control over the Niger basin and the acquisition of the coastal territories during the 1880s. Meanwhile, the Germans, acting as middlemen, staked out East and Southwest Africa. The Congo basin was raged over by four countries: Belgium, France, Britain, and Portugal. An agreement was reached among all the European powers in 1884–1885 at the Berlin Conference. It was a formalization of the colonial rule. At the conference, all the European powers met and partitioned Africa with the purpose to avoid future conflict among the European powers. King Leopold II of Belgium got the Congo Basin—the Congo Free State. Germany received East Africa (German East Africa or Tanganyika—modern Tanzania, Rwanda, and Burundi), Togoland, Cameroon, and Southwest Africa (Namibia). Portugal laid claims on Angola and Mozambique. Britain gained South Africa (including Rhodesia), Nigeria, the Gold Coast, and lands from Egypt to Kenya (including Egypt, Sudan, Kenya, and Uganda). France got Madagascar and most of West Africa. France had already occupied Algeria. Spain held Western Sahara and Spanish Guinea, while Italy received Lybia and Somaliland. The only two independent areas were Liberia and Ethiopia. Hence the period from 1880 to 1914 can be described as a period of conquest and establishing "presence" in Africa.

Name _____ Date _____

Challenges

1. Define imperialism.

_____

2. Define colonialism.

_____

3. Why is the first phase of European imperialism and colonialism in Africa known as the "scramble for Africa"?

_____

_____

4. Name the three motivating factors that led to the colonization of Africa.

_____

_____

5. What is ethnocentrism?

_____

6. Why did the Europeans feel it a duty and right to "civilize the Africans"?

_____

_____

7. Why did the Africans not resist violently the European "scramble for power"?

_____

_____

8. How was the partition of Africa decided among the European powers?

_____

9. Who were the European powers involved in the partition of Africa?

_____

10. Name the only two independent areas in Africa during this time.

_____

11. Describe briefly the period between 1880 and 1914 in Africa.

_____

Name _____ Date _____

Points to Ponder

1. Describe the partition of Africa in 1884–1885 among the European powers.

_____

_____

_____

_____

_____

2. From your knowledge of the previous chapters, why did the Europeans believe that the Africans were "uncivilized" and inferior?

_____

_____

_____

_____

_____

3. In what ways did the Europeans try to "civilize" the Africans?

_____

_____

_____

_____

_____

_____

Map Activity

Using Map 5 on page 87 as a resource, outline, color, and label on the blank activity map of Africa on page 89 the partition of Africa by the European powers by 1914.

Imperialism and Colonialism in Africa, Part 2, 1914–1945

African boundaries, established at the end of World War I, changed after World War II when Germany lost the war. The German territories were divided between France (Togoland), Britain (East Africa), and Belgium (Rwanda and Burundi).

The European powers established different types of rule in governing their colonies, depending on what their intentions were with their colonies. There were four approaches employed by the colonial powers: indirect rule, direct rule, company rule, and indirect company rule.

Lord Lugard

Indirect rule, first implemented by Lord Lugard in Nigeria and used by the British in West Africa, consisted of keeping the African power structure and making it a part of the colonial administration. If there was no local power structure, then new tribes and chiefs were created. The local leaders had to follow the colonial rules in return for protection, salaries, and gifts. The leaders were responsible for collecting taxes, providing cheap labor, and reporting back to the governor of the colony. The governor was an official appointed by the British government. The intent of the British was not to destroy the African structure and culture. They went to Africa to share their skills and values.

The French, Portuguese, and Germans preferred the system of **direct rule**. They imposed their rule onto the Africans. No powers were given to the Africans. The colonial government was made up of European officials or African officials appointed by the respective European governments. Each colonial territory was administrated by a governor-general.

Company rule was exercised by the Belgians. The Congo Free State was the personal domain of King Leopold II of Belgium, and his rule is known as the most brutal of all colonial rules. He gave Belgian businesses free access to the Congo, who administered the colony and exploited the mineral and human resources. The treatment of the Africans was so harsh that the Belgian government took possession of the territory in 1908, when it became known as the Belgian Congo. However, the Belgian businesses still ruled the colony.

Indirect company rule was adopted in Northern and Southern Rhodesia (now Zimbabwe and Zambia). It was implemented by a British entrepreneur, called Rhodes. In 1888, he set up his own private company, the British South Africa Company, after he acquired control of the gold and diamond resources of the area. Between 1890 and 1923, he and his company set up a colonial administration using the British system of indirect rule. In 1923, the company colony became self-governing and the white settler residents ran the administration, free from the control of the British government.

Name _____ Date _____

Challenges

1. What territories did Belgium receive from Germany after World War II?

_____

2. What area did Britain take over from Germany?

_____

3. France took over what territory after World War II?

_____

4. Where was indirect rule first implemented?

_____

5. In indirect rule, what were the local leaders responsible for?

_____

_____

6. How were Africans treated in a direct rule system?

_____

_____

7. Who administered the Congo Free State?

_____

8. Why did the Belgian government take possession of the Congo in 1908?

_____

9. Why type of rule was adopted in Rhodesia?

_____

10. Who ran the administration in Rhodesia when the colony became self-governing?

_____

_____

Name _____ Date _____

Points to Ponder

1. Describe the four kinds of rule that the European powers used to govern their respective colonies in Africa. List which of the European powers used which rule.

_____

_____

_____

_____

_____

_____

2. What is the difference between direct and indirect rule? Which one do you think is the better type of rule and why?

_____

_____

_____

_____

_____

_____

3. What is the difference between company and indirect company rule? Which one do you think is the better type of rule and why?

_____

_____

_____

_____

_____

Colonialism: Its Effects on Africa

The colonial powers adopted economic policies and practices that would destroy, rather than help, Africa economically, politically, and culturally in the future. The effects of colonialism, in fact, destroyed Africa's traditional lifestyles and culture. The European powers did not have Africa's interests in mind. They were only concerned with their own interests. The negative effects of colonialism became

Africans were forced to accept and serve the Europeans who came to establish colonies in Africa.

evident after the independence of many African countries.

The economic policies adopted by the European powers were several.

1. The colonial governments took much of the land away from the Africans for personal or commercial use, such as mining and large commercial farms. The Europeans took the best land and called it their own. It was Belgium and Britain in Central, East, and South Africa who were primarily responsible for this practice—the Belgians in Congo and the British in Kenya and South Africa. Because Central, East, and South Africa had pleasant climates and fertile soil for agriculture, the British and Belgians started to settle and immigrate into these areas.

2. Since the European powers needed manpower to manage their farms and mining companies, they used Africans as cheap labor. The Africans, either having lost their lands or not able to live off their lands, began to move to the towns, farms, or mines in search of work. The working conditions were horrible, often involving corporal punishment, and the wages were low, partially given in the form of cash and partially as food rations.

3. The colonial governments also needed money to pay for running these overseas governments and for services for the settler communities. Their mother countries in Europe gave the colonial governments little financial help, and so they needed to increase their capital by taxing the local Africans. This became a problem after World War II, when Europe was devastated and broke. Taxing the Africans went hand in hand with the use of African labor. Since taxes had to be paid in European currency, the Africans were indirectly forced to work for the Europeans in order to obtain the cash for paying the taxes. The result was that more and more Africans were forced to work for the Europeans.

4. Because of the loss of manpower after the two world wars, the European colonial powers started a new policy of forced labor, starting in the 1920s. Africans were recruited to work and sent to towns, farms, and mines. The results were many: African men were separated from their families, since only the men were used; villages lacked the manpower for food production, which led to famine; male homosexuality and female

prostitution increased among the African communities in the towns; and there was alienation from traditional village life, which led to the declining power of the village chiefs. In addition, immigrant laborers from Asia were employed by the Europeans, who were responsible for the local economy. This created tension between the Africans and the foreign immigrants.

5. The Europeans also changed the economic structure of African society. They introduced commercial or cash crops to meet the industrial demands in their home countries. Cocoa, coffee, tea, and cotton were produced on a large scale, and minerals were mined extensively. This resulted in neglecting the production of food for basic living. In turn, this neglect led to famine among many Africans. In short, the Europeans changed the economy from one where basic foods were produced to an economy based on the production of a few cash crops. All the crops produced were then exported to the home countries at the prices set by the colonies. In addition, there were few colonies that allowed Africans to grow these cash crops for their own benefit. Moreover, trade was not allowed between Africans. As a result, the Africans became producers of cash crops and minerals, which were exported to Europe.

6. The colonial powers had no plans to industrialize or aid in the modernization of Africa. Africa produced the raw materials, which were exported to Europe, re-exported to Africa as final products, and sold at high prices, which the Africans could not afford to pay.

Who benefited, then, from colonialism? Did it help or hurt the Africans? Many will admit that there were many negative results for the Africans, such as the following: resource depletion; labor exploitation; unfair taxation; lack of industrialization; dependence on cash crop economy; no trade allowed; the fragmentation of traditional African society, culture, and values; retarded political development; and ethnic rivalries within countries, since the boundaries were the ones set by Europeans. However, without colonialism, Africa would still today be behind the rest of the world in many areas. Some historians claim that there were some positive results.

1. Western medicine was introduced, which aided in the growth of the African population.
2. Formal education was introduced, which helped broaden the African outlook.
3. Africa's infrastructure was based on the European one with regard to the road system, railway, water, electricity, and communication systems.
4. The introduction of Christianity promoted literacy and health care through the work of missionaries. It created a basis for all Africans to come together and assist one another. Christianity made African spirituality simpler, such as in issues concerning life after death and the quest for salvation. There was no need for sacrifices and rituals, which were traditionally required. It made individual progress possible because it destroyed the traditional fabric of the African community.
5. The boundaries, as established by the different colonial powers, made state formation easier in the process of independence.

Name _____ Date _____

Challenges

1. Which European powers took much of the land of Central, East, and South Africa?

_____

2. Where did colonial governments get their money?

_____

3. Why did Africans move to towns, farms, and mines?

_____

_____

4. How were the Africans supposed to pay their taxes?

_____

5. Why were African men forced to work and sent to towns, farms, and mines?

_____

_____

6. How were Asian laborers introduced to Africa?

_____

7. Why were there famines in Africa when much of the land was being farmed?

_____

_____

8. Where were Africans expected to get manufactured goods?

_____

_____

9. Who helped promote literacy and health care in Africa?

_____

10. What infrastructure systems were made possible by the European powers?

_____

_____

_____

Name _____ Date _____

Points to Ponder

1. How did the European powers destroy Africa economically?

_____

_____

_____

_____

2. How did the European powers destroy Africa culturally?

_____

_____

_____

_____

3. Did the Africans benefit at all from European colonial rule? Why?

_____

_____

_____

_____

4. Do you think the benefits outweigh the negative results of colonialism? Why?

_____

_____

_____

_____

_____

South Africa, Part 1

Before the middle of the seventeenth century A.D., South Africa was inhabited in part by hunters and gatherers speaking the Khoisan language, called "Bushmen" or "Hottentots" in literature, and in part by farmers and herders speaking a variety of Bantu languages, which belong to the Niger-Congo language family. The Bantu-speaking people, during the Iron Age migrations, had reached South Africa by A.D. 300.

The modern history of South Africa starts in 1652, when the Dutch East India Company founded an outpost in Cape Town and settled 60 Dutch farmers. They farmed and raised animals to be sold to the traveling merchants as they passed on their way to Asia. The Dutch settlers became known as **Boers**, which means "farmers" in Dutch. By 1800, the Dutch settlers called themselves **Afrikaners** and developed a language called **Afrikaans**.

Not long after the Dutch had settled in Cape Town, they started waging war against the Khoisan-speaking people. They expanded their

Shaka Zulu

settlements into the interior, pushing northward from their cape settlements. The reason was greed. They wanted more land and, with it, more human labor. As they moved inland, they conquered the native people, subjecting and exploiting the Africans on their way. As the Boer population grew, they expanded eastward, displacing and subjecting the Khoisan people. By the late 1700s, the Boers had crossed the Orange River and started to fight the Bantu-speaking people. Unlike the Khoisan hunters and gatherers, the Bantu farmers and herders were able to defend themselves against the Boers, resulting in a series of wars of dispossession, known as the "Kaffir Wars." The year 1779 marks the beginning of these wars, which were to last for 100 years. Gradually, the white settlements expanded to the northeast. In 1795, the Dutch Boers had set up two Afrikaner Republics near the Cape of Good Hope, Graaff Reinet and Swellendam.

By 1800, the Afrikaners had also adopted their own ideology, which was to build a farming economy and social relationship on the basis that "all Africans were designed by God to labor as the white man's slaves."

Early in the nineteenth century, a new enemy, the British, reached the South African coast. The British took over the cape settlements from the Afrikaners in 1806 and established the Cape Colony. Their purpose was to abolish slave trade and the slave-based system of the Dutch. As the British pushed inland in a northward direction, they were drawn into warfare with the Bantu-speaking Africans.

In 1834, the British outlawed slavery in the Cape Colony with the result that one of the largest Afrikaner invasions into Natal and South Africa took place, known as the "Great

Trek" led by Louis Trichart. The "Great Trek" took place between 1835 and 1843. It resulted in the creation of the Natal Republic in 1838, but the British took it from the Dutch in 1843. During the 1850s, two Afrikaner Republics were founded, the Transvaal and the Orange Free State.

As the process of dispossession by the Dutch continued, another development was emerging on the east coast of Africa. Since the transatlantic slave trade was declining in the early nineteenth century, another export of slaves was developing on the east coast, which spread southward into South Africa. The east coast slaving resulted in the spread of violence and local warfare throughout the interior of Central and South Africa. Depopulation of this area was also widespread. It was common for some Bantu-speaking tribes to participate in the slave trade, most notably the Zulu. The Zulu went on slaving raids, capturing neighboring slaves for export on the east coast. They established a strong military state. Shaka became the leader of the Zulu nation and kingdom in 1818. His military tactics led the Zulu to the conquest of large areas in southeast Africa. The Zulu was to become a very powerful enemy to the British.

After 1830, the British, planning overall control of South Africa, fought against two enemies, the Africans, chiefly the Zulu, and the Dutch Boers. In 1879, the British invaded the Zulu Kingdom under Ceshwayo, Shaka's successor, and ended their power. The war against the Boers was called the Anglo-Boer War and was fought between 1899 and 1902. The Dutch Boers were defeated. The war ended with a peace, called the Peace of Vereeniging (which means "Peace of the Union").

In 1902, the country was handed to a white minority, including both English-speaking and Afrikaans-speaking communities. The white minority was granted the limitless subjugation of blacks, and there was also free availability to the whites of black-owned labor and black labor.

In 1910, South Africa took formal shape with the Act of the Union. The two British colonies of the Cape and Natal and the two Afrikaner Republics of Transvaal and Orange Free State were united. The British government left the country, and South Africa was now a separate country subjugated by a racist rule of "whites only." In 1948, this system of rule was to be called "**Apartheid**."

Apartheid—lit. "separateness" (in Afrikaans); a political system which existed in South Africa describing the relationship between the whites on the one hand, and the blacks and colored Africans on the other hand. It was a racist rule of "whites only," and the country was governed by laws in their making and application of which the black majority, including colored Africans of mixed origin, was to be allowed no voice. The African blacks and colored people were seen as inferior and were humiliated and degraded by the dominant, power-holding whites.

Name _____ Date _____

Challenges

1. Who settled in South Africa during the seventeenth century?

_____

2. What did the Boers call themselves by 1800?

_____

3. What were the "wars of dispossession" between the Dutch Boers and Africans called?

_____

4. Which European power rivaled the Dutch in South Africa during the nineteenth century?

_____

5. What is the "Great Trek"?

_____

_____

6. Who led the "Great Trek"?

_____

7. Which Bantu-speaking tribe did the British fight during the nineteenth century?

_____

8. Who made the Zulu nation a powerful military state?

_____

9. What factor led to the rise of the Zulu Kingdom?

_____

_____

10. What war was fought between the Afrikaners and the British from 1899 to 1902?

_____

11. When did South Africa formally take shape?

_____

Name _____ Date _____

Points to Ponder

1. Describe the relationship between the Dutch Boers and the British in South Africa during the nineteenth and early twentieth centuries.

_____

_____

_____

_____

_____

_____

2. Briefly describe the Apartheid system of rule. What events and ideologies led to the formalization of this system of rule in 1948?

_____

_____

_____

_____

_____

_____

3. Why are the "Kaffir Wars" known as the wars of dispossession? Who and what did the Dutch dispossess?

_____

_____

_____

_____

_____

South Africa, Part 2

After the Act of the Union in 1910, the white settlers had control in South Africa. They set up a political system in which they had complete political control over the Africans. Discrimination against non-whites was secured by the formalization of a set of laws and segregation of the Africans in the areas of education, politics, and territory. The Mines and Works Act of 1911 limited skilled mining jobs to whites and coloreds (people of mixed racial background) only. Later this law was extended to include the skilled jobs in the building industry. In 1913, the Natives Land Act divided the land between the Africans and the Europeans. Only 13 percent of the land, called "reserves," was given to the

Nelson Mandela

Africans. Other laws limited the movement of African workers in certain areas, such as the gold and diamond mining areas. The Africans were left with no political or economic rights, leading to the segregation of blacks and whites throughout South Africa in every aspect of life. In 1948, the National Party of the Afrikaners formally established this racist rule of "whites only" and called it "Apartheid."

More laws were enacted to keep this Apartheid system in place. In 1949, the Prohibition of Mixed Marriages Act passed, forbidding marriages between whites and non-whites. In 1950, the Population Registration Act passed, securing every South African as a member of a specific racial social group: white, colored, or black. The Group Areas Act in 1957, amended in 1966, created separate residential areas within cities and towns according to race. This led to the relocation of many Africans into designated neighborhoods. A notable law was passed in 1959. The Natives Land Act of 1913 was extended to a new law known as the Promotion of Bantu-Self-Governing Act. The Africans were ethnically divided into eight distinct national groups. Each group was assigned a "reserve," called bantustans or homelands, each controlled by a local traditional chief. There were 10 homelands, including the KwaZuku homeland of the Zulu, the Transkei homeland of the Xhosa people, and the KwaNdebele homeland of the Ndebele. Other laws regulated the movement of Africans within the urban areas, segregated all educational and social facilities, banned the formation of trade unions, and censored any publicity against Apartheid.

The history of South Africa during the Apartheid Era was full of protests, strikes, and boycotts, often bloody and violent. Starting in the 1950s, the African National Congress (ANC), a national African organization, tried to struggle for the rights and freedom of the Africans. Leaders in the struggle for freedom include Nelson Mandela and Steve Biko. In 1964, Mandela was imprisoned for 27 years for his involvement in the freedom movement as leader of the ANC. Biko was a student and became involved in student protests against the government. As leader of the South African Student Organization (SASO), he was tortured and imprisoned, and he died in in prison in 1977.

The struggle between the Africans and whites increased in the 1980s for several reasons. To the north, the Africans had gained independence in Angola, Mozambique, and Zimbabwe. This heightened nationalism in South Africa. South Africa became involved in a civil war with Namibia, who was seeking independence. The world was becoming aware of the racist and inhumane system of the South African government and started boycotting South Africa, producing a feeling of isolation among the whites. Economic sanctions were imposed by the United States and other Western countries in 1986, which caused problems. Furthermore, protests, strikes, and violent conflicts between the Africans and whites intensified dramatically in the late 1980s.

A fundamental change took place in 1989, when President Botha (ruled 1978–1989) resigned due to the problems South Africa was facing. The new president, F.W. de Klerk (ruled 1989–1994), led the way for the dismantling of Apartheid. Political prisoners were released from prison, including Nelson Mandela, in 1992. In 1991, a number of laws were repealed, including the Natives Land Act and Group Areas Act.

Finally, in 1994, general elections were held, and on May 10, Nelson Mandela became the president of South Africa and brought Apartheid to an end.

An abstract from Nelson Mandela's Inaugural Address follows (*The Boston Globe,* May 15, 1994, p. 74):

"...We are both humbled and elevated by the honor and privilege that you, the people of South Africa, have bestowed on us, as the first president of a united, democratic, non-racial, and non-sexist South Africa, to lead our country out of the valley of darkness.

We understand it still that there is no easy road to freedom.

We know it well that none of us acting alone can achieve success, reconciliation, for nation building, and for the birth of a new world.

Let there be justice for all.

Let there be peace for all.

Let there be bread, water, and salt for all.

Let each know that for each the body, mind, and the soul have been freed to fulfill themselves.

Never, never, never again shall it be that this beautiful land will again experience the oppression of one by another and suffer the indignity of being the skunk of the world.

The sun shall never set on so glorious a human achievement!

Let freedom reign. God bless Africa!"

Name _____ Date _____

Challenges

1. When was Apartheid established and by whom?

_____

_____

2. What were the ways in which the system of Apartheid was established and secured?

_____

_____

3. What did the Natives Land Act consist of?

_____

_____

4. Which two acts involved the territorial segregation of Africans from the whites?

_____

5. What is a South African "homeland"?

_____

6. What does the ANC stand for?

_____

7. Name two South African leaders who fought for the freedom of their country.

_____

8. In what way did the Africans fight the Apartheid system?

_____

_____

9. Which South African president started the dismantling of the Apartheid system?

_____

10. When and by whom was Apartheid abolished?

_____

_____

Name _____ Date _____

Points to Ponder

1. Name and describe the different laws enacted to establish and secure the system of Apartheid since the Act of the Union in 1910.

_____

_____

_____

_____

_____

_____

2. Do you think that Nelson Mandela should be regarded as one of the world's greatest politicians? Why?

_____

_____

_____

_____

_____

_____

3. After reading the abstract from Nelson Mandela's inaugural speech, describe how he felt as he was speaking. Try to read the passage as if you were Nelson Mandela.

_____

_____

_____

_____

_____

_____

Africa's Road to Independence

African Independence Leaders (left to right): Kenneth Kaunda (Zambia), Julius Nyerere (Tanzania), Jomo Kenyatta (Kenya), and Milton Obote (Uganda)

Africa's road to independence was due to nationalist movements by the Africans themselves. A number of factors were at work in the rise of African nationalism: colonial oppression; the role of the missionary churches; the effects of the two world wars; the Pan-African movement; the role of the League of Nations; and the role of the United Nations.

The colonial powers had exploited the Africans. The experience of most Africans was oppressive and negative. The Africans were degraded and humiliated, their land was confiscated, and they were used as cheap labor.

Missionary churches offered the Africans education. The education consisted of basic literacy and the teaching of the values of Western society. It also inspired the Africans to raise their level of productivity. The appetites of some Africans were whet for more education. These men went for further education abroad, and it provided them with the skills to voice their demands and question the legitimacy of colonialism. Some of these Africans were to become Africa's first leaders and the presidents of their countries after independence, such as Jomo Kenyatta of Kenya and Leopold Sedar Senghor of Senegal. The missionaries also brought the Africans the teachings of Christianity. These teachings contradicted the practices of the colonial powers and the missionary churches themselves. Christianity taught that everyone was equal in God's eyes, and hence everyone should be treated fairly and equally. But, in practice, this was not the case. The churches were racist and did not criticize colonial rule. In fact, they even looked down upon African culture and values and tried to destroy them. So the missionary churches gave the Africans the education to fight for their freedom, and it led to the rise of the independent African churches.

During World Wars I and II, millions of African soldiers who had fought for the colonial powers had died. Those who survived had learned modern military skills, but what angered the Africans was the lack of gratitude from the Europeans. The Africans felt that their countrymen had died in vain for a cause they did not even understand. They saw for the first time that the white man was not superior to the black man, but the same. The military skills acquired from fighting assisted the nationalistic movements. Moreover, the rise of unemployment and the decline of economic conditions, such as overcrowded cities,

71

inadequate health and educational facilities, the increase in taxes, and forced labor were all effects of the world wars, especially World War II. The European powers, exhausted financially and militarily and tired of war, were unwilling or unable to fight the nationalistic movements.

Pan-Africanism was an ideology that had two major elements: the common heritage of people of African descent throughout the world, and the obligation of the Africans to work for the cause of one another elsewhere. It originated in a meeting held in London in 1900 by Sylvester Williams. Many conferences followed that were organized by W.E.B. DuBois, and the first of five was held in Paris in 1919. The last of the conferences was held in Manchester, England, in 1945. This was the most important conference of all; first, because more Africans were involved than before, including future presidents who would lead their countries to independence, such as Kwame Nkrumah of Ghana and Jomo Kenyatta of Kenya. Second, there were reports on the horrible conditions of the Africans. Third, the Africans demanded reforms to improve the condition of the people, including a decent wage and health care. Finally, the idea of independence was expressed. Thus, Pan-Africanism changed from being a protest movement against racism to a tool of African national movements fighting for self-rule. The unity of all Africans and the hope for the development of a future All-African federation led to the development in 1963 of the Organization of African Unity (OAU).

The role of the League of Nations and the United Nations Organization accounted in part for furthering independence movements in Africa. The League of Nations was founded after World War I in order to avoid another major war in Europe. It had mandated Germany's territories in Africa to become mandate territories of the allied powers, with the purpose to eventually grant independence to them. The weakness of the league, however, led to World War II. After World War II, the United Nations Organization (UN) was founded. Its goal was to promote respect and observance of human rights of all people. Colonialism was unacceptable in the international community, and Africa had the right to govern itself. So the UN was used by independence movements in African countries. Socialist countries provided moral and material assistance in the form of weapons in the support for freedom.

African nationalism began to assert itself after World War II. The activists consisted of lawyers, doctors, professional groups, merchants, urban workers, and farmers. The national struggle was waged by religious associations, trade unions, political parties, welfare organizations, and youth groups.

The period after World War II from 1945 to 1965 is known as the period of decolonization and independence. This began with the independence of Ghana in 1957 in West Africa. Within a period of 10 years, most colonies of the French and British empires had gained their independence. The last two countries in Africa to become independent were Namibia in 1990 from South Africa and Eritrea in 1993 from Ethiopia.

Name _____ Date _____

Challenges

1. What education was offered by missionaries?

_____

_____

2. When Africans gained further education abroad, what was the result?

_____

_____

3. Name two of Africa's first leaders of independent nations.

_____

_____

4. Where did Africans gain military experience and skills?

_____

5. Why were the European powers unable or unwilling to fight the African nationalist movements after World War II?

_____

_____

6. Where and when was the first meeting of the Pan-African movement?

_____

7. Where and when was the most important Pan-African conference?

_____

8. What organization was formed in 1963 as a result of African national movements?

_____

9. What was the goal of the United Nations?

_____

_____

10. What dates generally mark the period of decolonization and independence?

_____

Name _____ Date _____

Points to Ponder

1. Explain how colonial oppression and the role of the missionary churches were influential in the African independence movements.

_____

_____

_____

_____

2. How did the two world wars and the role of the United Nations affect the African independence movements? Why?

_____

_____

_____

_____

_____

3. What is the Pan-African movement and how did it develop? Did it play a major role in the African independence movements? Why?

_____

_____

_____

_____

4. Which of the five factors that led to the rise of African nationalism do you think was most influential in the African independence movements? Why?

_____

_____

_____

_____

Independence and After

The transfer of power of the African colonies from the European colonists was, for the most part, achieved peacefully. However, there were some countries where independence was attained through violence and the loss of many lives, such as in Algeria, Namibia, Mozambique, Angola, Zimbabwe, and Kenya.

The speed of decolonization depended on the European powers and the areas they controlled. In British and French West Africa, the decolonization process and the transfer of power was achieved rapidly. After World War II, the British allowed the Africans to be part of the colonial government. New governmental institutions were set up, and national political parties were formed. Multi-party elections were also held. The first British colony in Africa to gain independence was Ghana in 1957, under Kwame Nkrumah. Like a domino effect, the rest of the British colonies followed. Between 1960 and 1968, all the former British colonies, except

**Robert Mugabe,
President of Zimbabwe**

for Southern Rhodesia, gained their independence, including Kenya under Jomo Kenyatta (see list, p. 6–7). This turning point in African history was called "a wind of change" by the British prime minister.

In the French territories, the French used the process of **assimilation**, which meant giving French citizenship to the Africans in their colonies and offering Africans the opportunity to participate in the French government. The idea of assimilation was resented in North Africa and Madagascar, which led to rebellions. France gave Tunisia and Morocco their independence in 1955–1956, but they did not grant independence to Algeria, which caused an anti-colonial rebellion (1954–1961). As a result, the French president, Charles de Gaulle, decided to let the colonies choose what they wanted, independence or being a member of a new French community controlled from Paris. In 1958, Guinea voted for independence, and by 1960, all other French colonies, including Madagascar, had gained independence (see list, p. 6–7). Belgium conceded independence to Zaire in 1960.

The areas which had not gained independence by 1968 belonged to Portugal and Spain. Only Djibouti still belonged to France until 1977, and Southern Rhodesia belonged to Britain and the white settlers until 1980. The Portuguese faced national resistance, which led to many years of long and painful wars until the mid-1970s, resulting in the independence of Angola, Mozambique, Guinea-Bissau, and Cape Verde in 1974–1975. But the independence of the Portuguese colonies upset the balance of power in South Africa and led to anti-colonial violence in Southern Rhodesia. It became independent in 1980 and became known as Zimbabwe. This led to Namibia wanting independence from South Africa. In 1990, after a long, bloody struggle, South Africa granted them independence. The last country to gain independence in Africa was Eritrea, which gained independence from Ethiopia in 1993.

After independence, when the nationalist leaders and their parties took over the power from the Europeans, there were many problems that the Africans inherited that affected African history and still affect Africa to this day. The problems include economic instability, territorial and ethnic divisions, and the non-realization of the people's high expectations for national development. As a result, all the African countries were afflicted with political instability. The situation has not changed much in the 1990s.

African national leaders made promises to the people, such as good jobs, decent housing, health care, and free education. However, there were not enough jobs, housing, or money. Many Africans were disappointed. All the land was bought by rich Africans, primarily politicians; hence, there was not enough land to redistribute to the people. In addition, most Africans were illiterate; there were not enough resources for education, so most Africans stayed illiterate.

Economically, the Africans had for a long time depended on the export of a few cash crops, such as coffee, cocoa, cotton, and metals. Hence, they heavily depended on European markets. Africa had become part of the world economy. Prices for the goods lowered, which resulted in the need to produce more crops to compete with the lower prices. This made it more difficult for Africans to grow crops. Even though the Africans were able to use the roads, telephones, and electrical systems, which the Europeans had set up during colonial times, the lack of new, advanced technology and technological knowledge among the Africans led to uneven development in most African nations.

Africa was traditionally divided into nearly 2000 ethnic groups, each with its own language and culture. The artificial boundaries set by the colonial powers were used to divide the African countries. These were boundaries that had taken no account of the different ethnic groups. For example, the Maasai were divided between Kenya and Tanzania. In other instances, one country was composed of different ethnic groups, such as Sudan and Nigeria. This led to fragmentation, political instability, and civil wars. An example of a civil war as a result of different ethnic groups living in the same country is found in Nigeria. Nigeria is divided between three main groups: the Yoruba in the West, the Ibo in the East, and the Muslim Hausa in the North. Rwanda, Burundi, and Sudan are more recent examples where civil strife has led to political and economic destruction.

Political instability is characterized by the personal greed and corruption inherent with the political leaders themselves. It has led to dictatorships and one-party rules throughout much of Africa. The national leaders accepted and followed the Marxist-Leninist perspective of history. This meant that the welfare of a state was ruled by a one-party structure. This led to over 70 military **coup d'etats** (a forcible overthrow of a government) between 1952 and 1968, 20 of which led to new army-led governments. This has continued into the 1990s. A recent example is Zaire, which was renamed the Democratic Republic of the Congo in 1997.

Name _____ Date _____

Challenges

1. What did the British prime minister mean by "a wind of change," describing the time between 1960 and 1968?

_____

_____

2. What country was the first British colony to gain independence in West Africa in 1957?

_____

3. What country was the first French colony to gain independence in West Africa in 1958?

_____

4. Which British colony had not gained independence by 1968?

_____

5. Which French colony had not gained independence by 1968?

_____

6. To which country did Namibia belong before gaining independence in 1990?

_____

7. To which country did Eritrea belong before gaining independence in 1993?

_____

8. What was the result of the independence of the Portuguese colonies in the mid-1970s?

_____

_____

9. Which countries experienced violence and a loss of lives in their struggle for independence?

_____

_____

10. After independence, why was there much civil strife in the African countries?

_____

_____

_____

Name _____ Date _____

Points to Ponder

1. Why was the time between 1960 and 1968 known as "a wind of change," a major turning point in African history?

_____

_____

_____

_____

2. Discuss the problems that African countries faced after gaining their independence.

_____

_____

_____

_____

3. Did the decolonization process and transfer of power proceed smoothly and rapidly throughout Africa? Why or why not?

_____

_____

_____

_____

Essay

Find an article on the political and economic situation of a specific African country in a popular magazine, such as *Time* or *Newsweek*, within the last 10 years. Summarize the article and detail the problems that the specific country you chose is experiencing.

Map Activity

On the blank activity map of Africa on page 89, using the list of countries on pages 6–7 and Map 6 on page 88, color the countries of Africa according to their dates of independence. Divide the countries up into the following groups: independence gained between 1950–1959, 1960–1969, 1970–1979, 1980–onwards. Use a different color for each group.

Traditional African Culture and Society

Africa consists of many different ethnic groups, each with its own language, traditions, and culture. But all Africans share the same history of oppression and exploitation by Europeans.

There are some general elements that characterize African society and culture, such as the structure of society, marriage rules, and religious beliefs.

The basic unit of any society is the social group. In Africa, there are three different types: those based on kinship, those based on skill or age, and those based on residence.

Kinship means the relationship between people through birth or marriage. One's descent is determined either through one's father or other male ancestors, known as **patrilineal descent**, or through the male relatives on the mother's side, known as **matrilineal descent**. In modern Africa, because of intermarriage, it is becoming more common to trace oneself through both parents, known as **bilineal descent**, which is common in Western

This Frafra man displays facial scarification. The patterns are designed according to ethnic group, region, and personal style.

societies. Descent is important because it gives a person his or her identity within society and determines inheritance and residence. For example, in patrilineal descent groups, boys have the rights of inheritance and are identified with the father's community.

The most common type of family unit in Africa is the extended family, which includes one's immediate family and relatives as far back as three generations, often living in close proximity to one another. Family ties and relationships are very important among Africans. The family is more important than the individual. The family takes care of the training and education of its children and takes care of the elders, who are respected because of their age and wisdom. In contrast, the basic family unit in Western society is the nuclear family, which consists of the immediate family, meaning the mother, father, and children. Western society stresses the individual rather than the community.

Every individual belongs to the family and the community as a whole. The individual in African society goes through distinct stages of life; for example, infancy, childhood, adulthood, and marriage. Each stage is celebrated by elaborate rituals involving the community. A young person going into adulthood is marked by an initiation ceremony. In general, for boys this involves circumcision. Sometimes circumcision is also performed on girls going into womanhood. Other practices include the scarring of the skin or body tattoos.

Marriage is very important and has a greater societal significance in African societies than in Western societies. In Africa, although marrying for love is not ruled out and is becoming more common in modern African society, there are other, more important reasons for marriage. Marriages are important to uphold social traditions, to ensure the survival of the family, to maintain higher status within the society, and to enforce political and economic alliances between different kinship groups. Marriage is a relationship between two extended families, rather than a man and a woman, and is often arranged by the families. Part of the marriage ceremony involves the transfer of property to either the bride's family, known as a **dowry**, or to the groom's family, known as the **bridewealth**. Families discuss how much property, in the form of cattle, weapons, or money, should be given in order for the marriage to take place. Whereas, in Western society sexual fidelity is expected between both partners, in African society this is not a necessary condition. For many African societies, **polygamy** is a preferred form of marriage. Polygamy means that either the husband can marry multiple wives, known as **polygyny**, or a woman can marry multiple men, known as **polyandry**. Of the two forms of polygamy, polygyny is preferred by, used in, and accepted morally by the Christian church in Africa. As a result, extramarital affairs are more prevalent among Africans. The reasons for the origin and common occurrence of polygyny are several. It provides social and economic stability within the family, it helps in the inheritance of property, and it is associated with wealth and prestige within African societies. Another factor that led to this practice was the high infant mortality rate, which means that more children need to be born to ensure the survival of the family.

African religious traditions are characterized by several elements. The first element consists of the belief in the concept of God, of a supreme being, who created the universe. This supreme deity is assisted by lesser deities, often tied to nature, such as the God of Rain, the God of the Sea, the God of the Forest, and the God of Fertility. These deities often take on a physical human form. The second element consists of the belief in spirits. Spirits are a force of life, but they have no physical form. The Africans believe that everything in nature, such as a tree or a rock, has a spirit. There are also human spirits, which consist of those people who have died. This belief in spirits is known as **animism**.

Africans strongly believe in their ancestors, who are intermediaries between the God and the community. They believe that the community includes not only the living but also the dead; hence, ancestor worship is a very important part of the traditional religious belief.

Part of African religion includes elaborate rituals, often including song and dance, to appease the gods, spirits, and ancestors. Africans also pray to the supernatural to aid them in the welfare of their society. Each society has a **shaman**, who is a part-time religious specialist. A shaman is an intermediary between the supernatural and the community. He or she has special powers and is able to contact the beyond by going into a trance or hypnotic state. A shaman is also the healer and helps the sick within the society.

Name _____ Date _____

Challenges

1. What is the basic family unit in African societies?

_____

2. What is the basic family unit in Western societies?

_____

3. Define kinship.

_____

_____

4. Why is kinship important?

_____

_____

5. What is the difference between patrilineal and bilineal descent?

_____

_____

6. What is polygyny?

_____

7. Why is polygamy a preferred from of marriage in African societies?

_____

_____

8. What is animism?

_____

9. Name three characteristics of traditional African religious beliefs.

_____

_____

10. What role does the shaman have in African societies?

_____

_____

Name _____ Date _____

Points to Ponder

1. Describe briefly the traditional African religious beliefs.

_____

_____

_____

_____

_____

_____

2. What is marriage in African societies? Describe briefly the different reasons for marriage in African society.

_____

_____

_____

_____

_____

_____

3. Compare the African structure of society, marriage rules, and religion to those of Western society.

_____

_____

_____

_____

_____

_____

Name _____ Date _____

Map 1: Africa and the Mediterranean

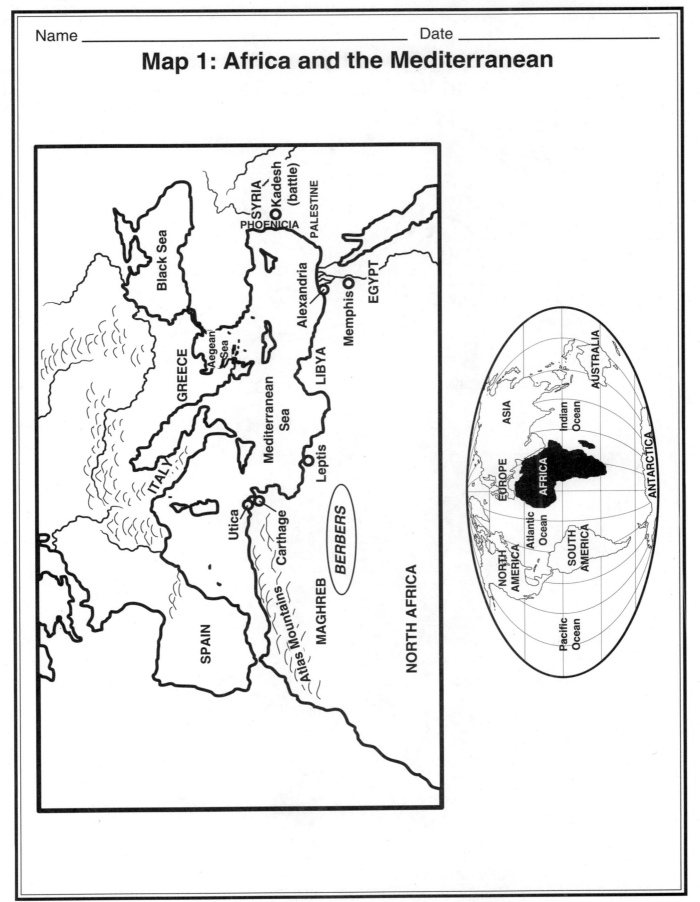

Name _____   Date _____

Map 2: African Physical Features and Vegetation Regions

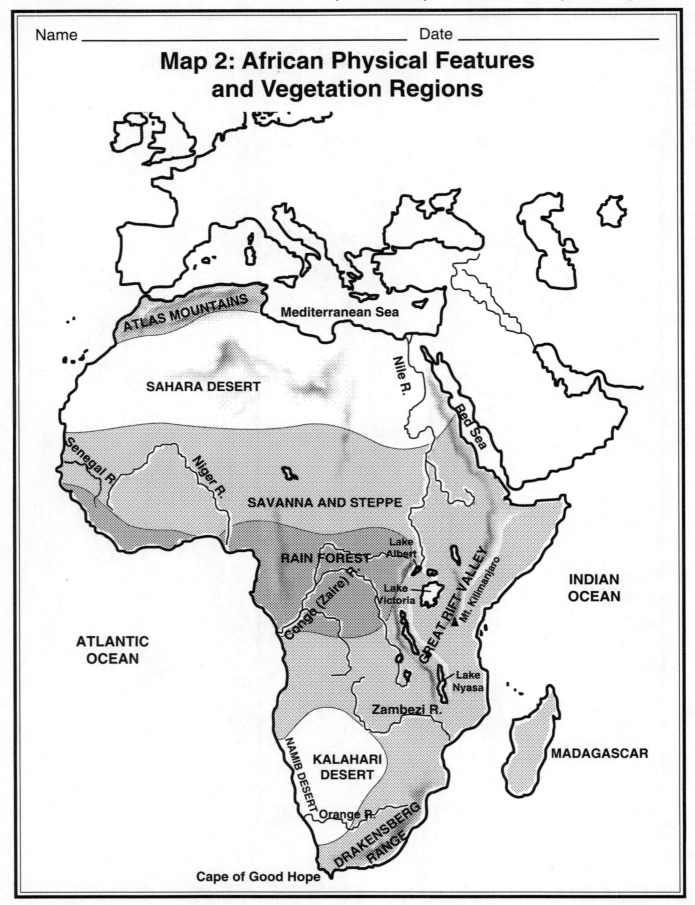

Name _____ Date _____

Map 3: The Regions of Africa

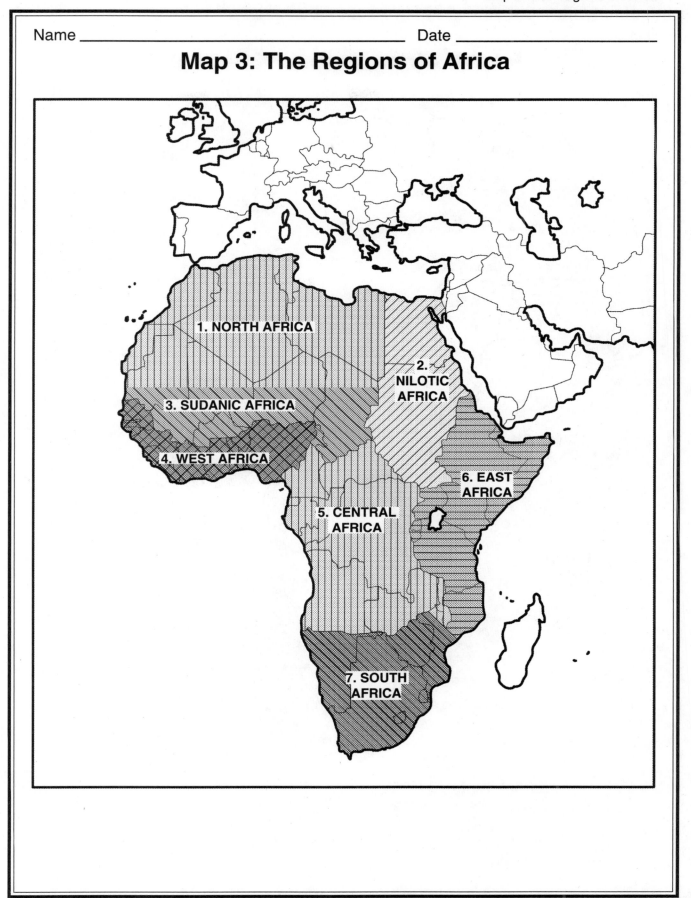

1. NORTH AFRICA

2. NILOTIC AFRICA

3. SUDANIC AFRICA

4. WEST AFRICA

5. CENTRAL AFRICA

6. EAST AFRICA

7. SOUTH AFRICA

Africa

Map 4: Africa, ca. A.D. 900–1800

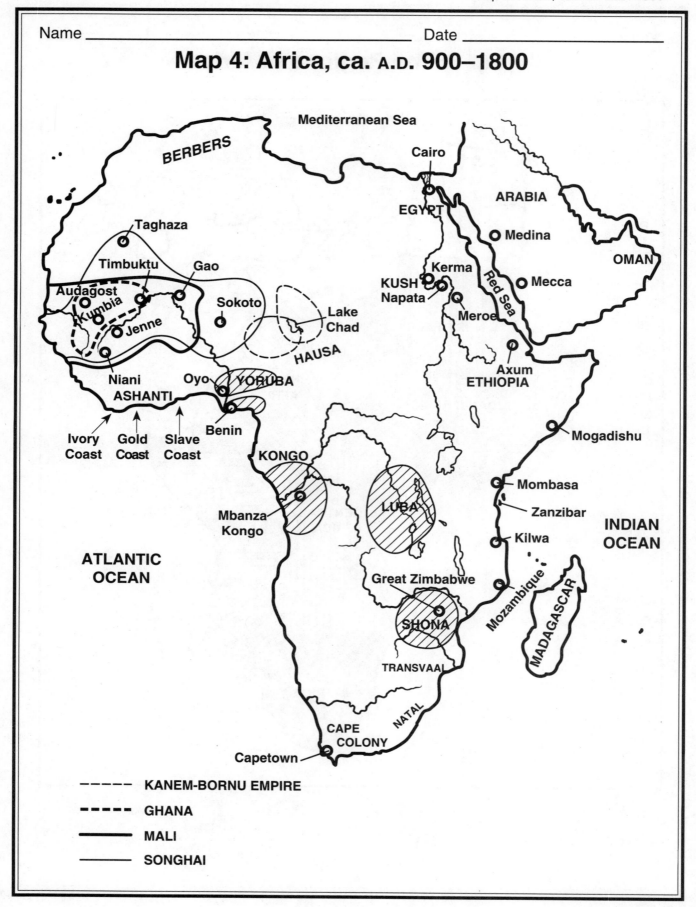

Name _____ Date _____

Map 4: Africa, ca. A.D. 900–1800

Mediterranean Sea

BERBERS

Cairo

ARABIA

EGYPT

Medina

OMAN

Taghaza

Kerma

Mecca

Timbuktu   Gao

KUSH
Napata

Red Sea

Audagost

Sokoto

Meroe

Kumbia

Lake
Chad

Jenne

HAUSA

Axum
ETHIOPIA

Niani
ASHANTI

Oyo   YORUBA

Benin

Mogadishu

Ivory
Coast

Gold
Coast

Slave
Coast

KONGO

Mombasa

Zanzibar

INDIAN
OCEAN

Mbanza
Kongo

LUBA

Kilwa

ATLANTIC
OCEAN

Great Zimbabwe

SHONA

TRANSVAAL

MADAGASCAR

Mozambique

NATAL

CAPE
COLONY

Capetown

– – – – – KANEM-BORNU EMPIRE

▪ ▪ ▪ ▪ ▪ GHANA

━━━━━ MALI

───── SONGHAI

Name _____   Date _____

Map 5: The Partition of Africa, 1880–1914

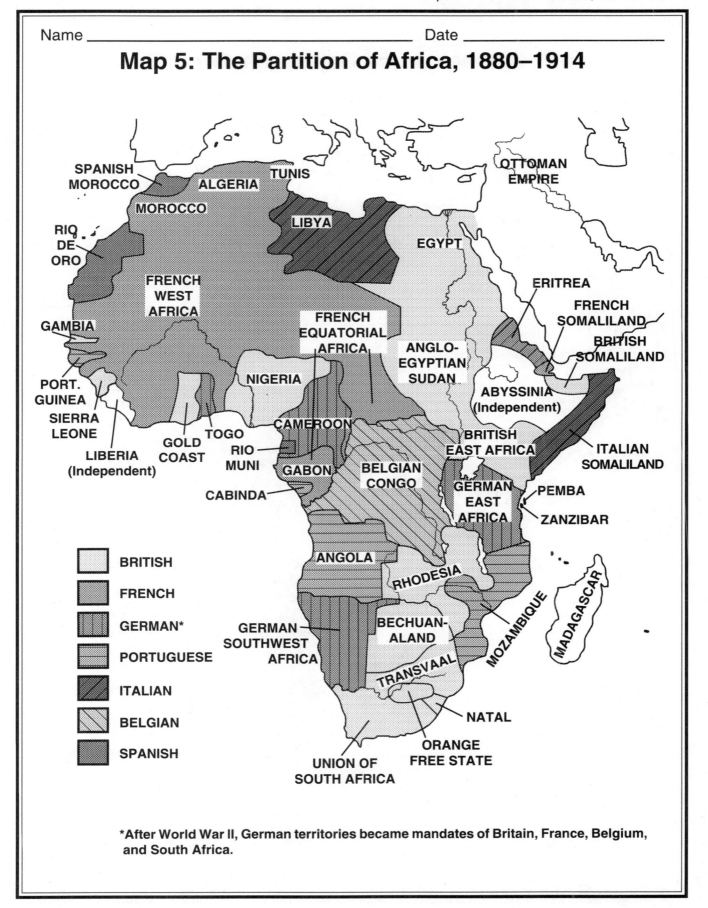

Legend:
- BRITISH
- FRENCH
- GERMAN*
- PORTUGUESE
- ITALIAN
- BELGIAN
- SPANISH

SPANISH MOROCCO
ALGERIA
TUNIS
OTTOMAN EMPIRE
MOROCCO
LIBYA
EGYPT
RIO DE ORO
ERITREA
FRENCH WEST AFRICA
FRENCH SOMALILAND
BRITISH SOMALILAND
GAMBIA
FRENCH EQUATORIAL AFRICA
ANGLO-EGYPTIAN SUDAN
PORT. GUINEA
NIGERIA
ABYSSINIA (Independent)
SIERRA LEONE
CAMEROON
ITALIAN SOMALILAND
LIBERIA (Independent)
GOLD COAST
TOGO
RIO MUNI
BRITISH EAST AFRICA
GABON
BELGIAN CONGO
GERMAN EAST AFRICA
PEMBA
ZANZIBAR
CABINDA
ANGOLA
RHODESIA
MADAGASCAR
GERMAN SOUTHWEST AFRICA
BECHUAN-ALAND
MOZAMBIQUE
TRANSVAAL
NATAL
UNION OF SOUTH AFRICA
ORANGE FREE STATE

*After World War II, German territories became mandates of Britain, France, Belgium, and South Africa.

Name _____ Date _____

Map 6: Independence Dates and Africa Today

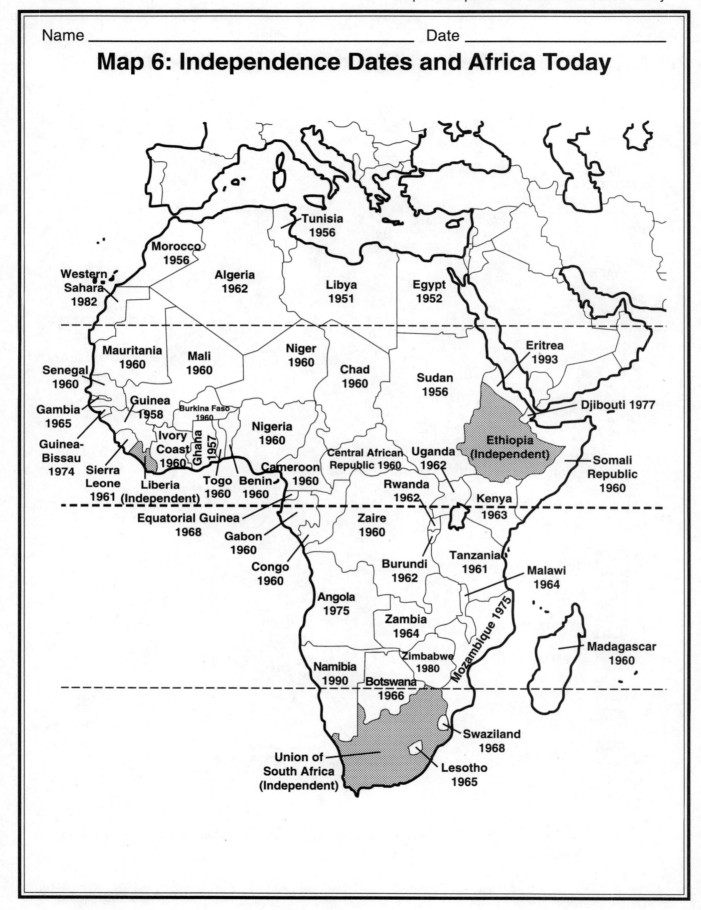

Tunisia
1956

Morocco
1956

Western
Sahara
1982

Algeria
1962

Libya
1951

Egypt
1952

Eritrea
1993

Mauritania
1960

Mali
1960

Niger
1960

Chad
1960

Sudan
1956

Djibouti 1977

Senegal
1960

Gambia
1965

Guinea
1958

Burkina Faso
1960

Nigeria
1960

Central African
Republic 1960

Uganda
1962

Ethiopia
(Independent)

Somali
Republic
1960

Guinea-
Bissau
1974

Ivory
Coast
1960

Ghana
1957

Sierra
Leone
1961

Liberia
(Independent)

Togo
1960

Benin
1960

Cameroon
1960

Rwanda
1962

Kenya
1963

Equatorial Guinea
1968

Gabon
1960

Zaire
1960

Burundi
1962

Tanzania
1961

Malawi
1964

Congo
1960

Angola
1975

Zambia
1964

Mozambique 1975

Namibia
1990

Zimbabwe
1980

Botswana
1966

Madagascar
1960

Swaziland
1968

Union of
South Africa
(Independent)

Lesotho
1965

Name _____ Date _____

Africa: Activity Map

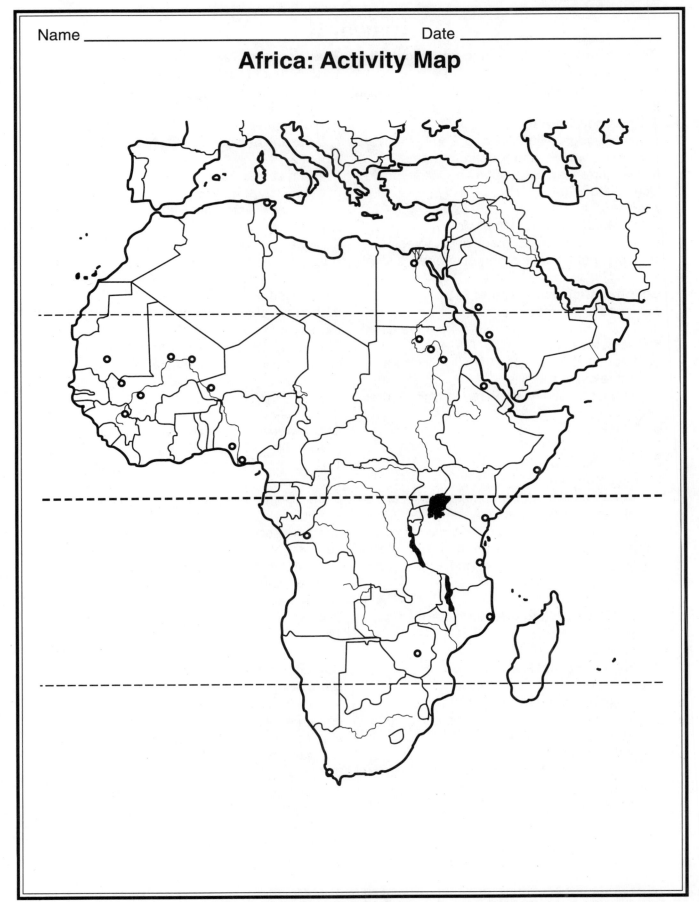

Answer Key

Geography and Its Influence on African History (page 10)
1. East African Rift Valley
2. Nile River
3. Egyptian Civilization
4. Nile, Senegal, Niger, Congo, Zambezi Rivers
5. Sahara, Namib, and Kalahari Deserts
6. Mediterranean Sea, Atlantic Ocean, Indian Ocean, Red Sea
7. seven
8. 20° North and South Latitude
9. deserts, woodlands, grasslands, forests
10. ivory, gold, iron, copper, diamonds, salt

Egyptian Civilization (page 14)
1. Menes or Narmer
2. The Egyptian writing system, from the Greek for "secret writings"
3. about 5000 B.C.., along the Nile River Valley
4. as "the gift of the Nile"
5. civil war, invasions, poverty, famine, oppression
6. Hittites
7. Hyksos
8. Sea People
9. Roman empire
10. urban society with a complex political and social structure and writing system
11. Egypt was urban, had a centralized government with the pharaoh as the absolute ruler, a hierarchical social structure, and a writing system.

North Africa Until the Seventh Century A.D. (page 17)
1. Berbers
2. Phoenicians and Romans
3. Carthage
4. Trans-Saharan trade
5. Roman coastal cities served as markets; introduction of the camel
6. gold, ivory, and slaves
7. The decline of Roman empire; invasions into North Africa
8. The rise and spread of Islam

The Rise and Spread of Islam in North and East Africa (page 21)
1. "to surrender" to the will of Allah
2. the prophet Mohammed
3. Mohammed's flight from Mecca to Medina
4. It was the beginning of the Muslim calendar in A.D. 622.
5. Islam spread to North Africa into Spain and into Asia as far as India.
6. political disintegration and the formation of separate political identities
7. any of the following: Timbuktu, Jenne, Gao, Audagost, Kumbi
8. any of the following: Kilwa, Mombasa, Mogadishu, Zanzibar
9. the revival and expansion of commerce; the formation of powerful states
10. any of the following: Mali, Songai, Kanem-Bornu, Benin in West Africa; Kongu, Luba in west-central Africa; Zimbabwe in southeast Africa

Sub-Saharan Civilizations: Kush and Axum (page 25)
1. Kingdom of Napata and Kingdom of Meroe
2. Axum
3. the control over the gold resources
4. Adulis
5. trade access to the Red Sea and a firm agricultural base
6. prime location for trade and rich in iron ores
7. King Ezana
8. Assyrians
9. iron
10. Egypt

Sub-Saharan Civilizations: The Sudanic Empires (page 29)
1. A state is a political system with a centralized government, a military force, a civil service, a stratified society of rulers and ruled, and literacy.
2. Ghana, Mali, Songhai, Kanem-Bornu
3. Kumbi
4. invasions from the north and west
5. Sundiata Keita
6. Niani
7. from the Atlantic north to the Sahara and east into central Sudan
8. invasion from Morocco

9. Kanem-Bornu
10. around Lake Chad

Sub-Saharan Civilizations: Kingdoms and States South of the Sudan (page 33)
1. Benin, Yoruba, Kongo, Luba
2. Niger River
3. Congo River
4. Portuguese
5. pepper, gold, ivory, slaves
6. glass beads, cloth, weapons
7. Kingdom of Kongo
8. King Alfonso I
9. enslaving of his people
10. Mbanza

Sub-Saharan Civilizations: East Africa, A.D. 1000–1600 (page 36)
1. a city that is self-governing like a state
2. Arabs, Indians, Persians, Malaysians
3. ivory, incense, spices, gold, oils, iron, and slaves
4. glazed pottery, cloth, glass beads, and china
5. Portuguese
6. Swahili
7. Kilwa, Mombasa, Mogadishu, Zanzibar
8. Limpopo and Zambezi Rivers
9. agriculture, gold resources, trade
10. unknown; probably exhaustion of land for farming and a growing population

The Atlantic Slave Trade, Part 1 (page 44)
1. African slaves were captured, sold, and transported across the Atlantic to the Americas.
2. The discovery of Americas by the Portuguese and Spanish
3. about 11.5 million
4. eighteenth century (1701–1800)
5. Portuguese, Dutch, French, British
6. No; It occurred earlier along the east coast of Africa and within Africa.
7. They captured and procured slaves from their neighbors through war.
8. firearms, tobacco, alcohol, cotton
9. 1650–1850
10. The coming of the Industrial Revolution in Europe; European abolitionists fighting to make an end of the trade

The Atlantic Slave Trade, Part 2 (page 47)
1. Europeans
2. Strong, young males
3. The Kongo-Angola region
4. 400
5. Trade in cheap industrial goods
6. Cotton, metal, palm oil
7. The Yoruba Kingdom and the Asanti empire
8. In West African societies along the Niger Delta

Sudan and East Africa During the Eighteenth and Nineteenth Centuries (page 50)
1. A holy struggle or war for the Muslims
2. Ushman Dan Fodio
3. Muhammed Bello
4. West African pastoralists who were converted to Islam
5. Portuguese
6. Arab Muslims
7. Mungo Park, David Livingstone
8. Local rebellions and invasions from the north and south
9. The pursuit of science; to "civilize the Africans"; to introduce Christianity
10. An increase in local warfare and turmoil

Imperialism and Colonialism in Africa, Part 1, 1880–1914 (page 54)
1. The exercise of power by a state beyond its own boundaries
2. The administrative control by a state over other people
3. The major European powers were partitioning Africa among themselves.
4. Scientific interest, spread of Christianity, imperialism
5. The belief that one's own culture is superior to others
6. The Africans were less advanced technologically and led a simpler, "primitive" way of life.
7. They were dependent on the Europeans economically; they did not think of the consequences colonialism might bring.
8. The 1884–1885 Berlin Conference
9. Britain, France, Belgium, Portugal, Germany, Spain, Italy
10. Liberia and Ethiopia
11. It was a period of conquest and establishing a "presence."

Imperialism and Colonialism in Africa, Part 2, 1914–1945 (page 57)
1. Rwanda and Burundi
2. East Africa
3. Togoland
4. Nigeria
5. Collecting taxes, providing cheap labor, and reporting back to the governor of the colony
6. European rule was imposed on the Africans and they were given no powers.
7. Belgian businesses
8. The businesses were treating the Africans too harshly.
9. Indirect company rule
10. The white settler residents

Colonialism: Its Effects on Africa (page 61)
1. Belgium and Britain
2. From taxes placed on Africans
3. To find jobs because they lost their land or couldn't make a living off their land
4. In European currency
5. There was a manpower shortage after the two world wars.
6. Europeans brought them in.
7. Most of the land was used for cash crops, which were exported. No basic foods were being grown.
8. They had to buy them at high prices from Europe.
9. Christian missionaries
10. Road, railway, water, electricity, and communication systems

South Africa, Part 1 (page 65)
1. Dutch Boers
2. Afrikaners
3. Kaffir Wars
4. The British
5. The migration of Afrikaners into Natal and South Africa
6. Louis Trichart
7. Zulu
8. Shaka
9. East coast slave trade and slave raiding
10. Anglo-Boer War
11. 1910

South Africa, Part 2 (page 69)
1. In 1948 by the National Party of Afrikaners
2. Discrimination against non-whites was secured through the enactment of laws and segregation.
3. The division of the land among Africans and whites; Africans only received 13 percent of the land
4. The Group Areas Act in 1957 and the Promotion of Bantu-Self-Governing Act in 1959
5. A reserve for Africans of the same ethnic group
6. African National Congress
7. Nelson Mandela and Steve Biko
8. By means of protests, strikes, and violent conflicts with police
9. President F.W. de Klerk
10. In 1994 by President Nelson Mandela

Africa's Road to Independence (page 73)
1. Basic literacy and teaching the values of Western society
2. They gained the skills to voice their demands and question the legitimacy of colonialism.
3. Jomo Kenyatta of Kenya and Leopold Sedar Senghor of Senegal
4. World Wars I and II
5. They were exhausted financially and militarily, and they were tired of war.
6. London, 1900
7. Manchester, England, 1945
8. The Organization of African Unity (OAU)
9. To promote respect and the observance of human rights of all people
10. 1945–1965

Independence and After (page 77)
1. A large number of colonies gained independence from Britain within a short time.
2. Ghana
3. Guinea
4. Southern Rhodesia
5. Djibouti
6. South Africa
7. Ethiopia
8. There was anti-colonial rebellion within the British colony of Southern Rhodesia, followed by the South African colony of Namibia, leading to their independence.

9. Algeria, Namibia, Mozambique, Angola, Southern Rhodesia (Zimbabwe), Kenya

10. The artificial boundaries set by the colonial powers divided up the different ethnic groups into several countries or united them into one country.

Traditional African Culture and Society (page 81)

1. The extended family

2. The nuclear family

3. The relationship between people through birth and marriage

4. To determine one's descent

5. Patrilineal descent is tracing one's descent through the father or other male relatives; bilineal descent traces one's descent through both sets of parents.

6. One man marrying multiple women

7. To ensure the survival of the family; to maintain higher status; to uphold social traditions; to strengthen political and economic alliances between families

8. The belief in the spirits in nature

9. Belief in a supreme being; belief in spirits; belief in ancestors

10. The shaman is a religious leader and healer.

Selected References

General
Cambridge History of Africa, Cambridge, 1984.
Davidson, Basil. *Africa in History*. New York, 1991 (rev. ed.).
Gibbs, J.L. Jr. (ed.). *Peoples of Africa*. New York, 1965.
Idowu, E. Bolaji. *African Traditional Religion*. New York, 1975.
July, Robert W. *A History of the African People*. Waveland Press, Illinois, 1998 (5th ed.).
Khapoya, Vincent B. *The African Experience*. Prentice Hall, N.J., 1998 (2nd ed.).
Lamb, David. *The Africans*. New York, 1984.
Phillipson, David W. *African Archaeology*. Cambridge, 1993 (2nd ed.).
Reader, John. *Africa. A Biography of the Continent*. New York, 1997.
The Horizon History of Africa. American Heritage Publishing Co. Inc., New York, 1971.

Specific regions or time periods
Collins, Robert O. (ed.). *Historical Problems of Imperial Africa*. Princeton, 1994.
Curtin, Philip. *Africa Remembered. Narratives by West Africans from the Era of the Slave Trade*. Waveland Press, Illinois, 1997.
Davidson, Basil. *Modern Africa. A Social and Political History*. New York, 1994 (3rd ed.).
Esedebe, P. Olisanwuche. *Pan-Africanism. The Idea and Movement 1776-1963*. Washington D.C., 1982.
Mandela, Nelson. *The Struggle in My Life*. New York, 1986.
Mannix, D.P. and M. Cowley. *Black Cargoes. A History of the Atlantic Slave Trade 1518–1865*. New York, 1962.
Pakenham, Thomas. *The Scramble for Africa 1876–1912*. New York, 1991.
Thompson, Leonard. *The Political Mythology of Apartheid*. Yale University Press, 1985.
Thompson, Leonard. *A History of South Africa*. Yale University Press, 1990.
Worden, Nigel. *The Making of Modern South Africa*. Cambridge, 1995.

Novels
Achebe, Chinua. *Things Fall Apart*.
Paton, Alan. *Cry the Beloved Country*.

Journals
Africa Contemporary Record
Africa South of the Sahara
Foreign Affairs
The Journal of Modern African Studies